W9-AVN-780

YOU HAVE HEARD IT SAID

You Have Heard It Said

Events of Reconciliation

JONATHAN MCRAY

RESOURCE *Publications* · Eugene, Oregon

YOU HAVE HEARD IT SAID
Events of Reconciliation

Copyright © 2011 Jonathan McRay. All rights reserved. Except for brief quotations in critical publications or reviews, no part of this book may be reproduced in any manner without prior written permission from the publisher. Write: Permissions, Wipf and Stock Publishers, 199 W. 8th Ave., Suite 3, Eugene, OR 97401.

Resource Publications
An Imprint of Wipf and Stock Publishers
199 W. 8th Ave., Suite 3
Eugene, OR 97401

www.wipfandstock.com

ISBN 13: 978-1-61097-054-9

Manufactured in the U.S.A.

Contents

Foreword

RECONCILIATION IS a path that must be walked, a journey, full of ups and downs, valleys and hilltops. We are all commanded by God to undertake this journey, but unfortunately, not everyone heeds this call. Still, there are many courageous people actually set out to accomplish the difficult task of reconciliation, in this collection you will find some of their stories. For years Musalaha has been asked to document the personal stories of these brave people, the men, women, and youth who have answered the divine call for fellowship, but we have been hesitant.

We knew that it would be difficult for these people to share their stories, since this always involves a certain measure of vulnerability, opening up and exposing an intensely personal and private process to the outside world. Especially when dealing with such a contentious, divisive issue, this can be very scary, and we want first and foremost to protect our participants. However, we decided that a collection of personal stories would help encourage our participants and supporters, and offer a model for those interested in joining the reconciliation projects Musalaha operates.

Our goal for this project was twofold: first we wanted to allow the participants to speak freely and openly about the process of reconciliation, and to explain the healing and transformative experience in their own words. At the same time, we wanted to honestly assess the challenges, and difficulties that come from engaging in the process of reconciliation. We have no interest in presenting sugar-coated, "feel-good" stories about how wonderfully Israeli Messianic Jews and Palestinian Christians get along. A certain amount of editorial cuts were made to these stories, but overall the voice of the participants comes through. The disagreements, challenges and inconsistencies are in these stories, and in these reflections; out in the open for all to see. In order to maintain this delicate balance, we needed to find someone with knowledge of the conflict and all of its intricacies, sensitivity to the pain and suffering experienced on both sides, and a willingness to ask difficult questions and speak the truth in love. In Jonathan McRay, we found a writer possessing of all these qualities.

Jonathan came to our office armed with an incredible writing ability and an excitement for the project that was contagious. He was young, idealistic, and full of energy; and he was to make use of every bit of it as he traveled throughout Israel and Palestine, over the course of his five month stay. In conducting around 40 interviews with Musalaha participants, as well as attending a number of Musalaha events, Jonathan was able to gain an understanding of what we, as an organization, stand for; the challenges we face and the issues we deal with. He also had to struggle with these same issues, and he displayed a generous spirit, and was able to relate to the people he encountered on a human level. This shows through in his stories and it shows through in his life.

Unfortunately, not all of these interviews became stories, and not all of the stories are included in this book. While every story is unique, important, and needs to be told, that would require a much bigger book. This volume is only a sample, but the stories it contains, and the reflections on the stories near the end, are representative of the restorative as well as difficult aspects of the journey of reconciliation. Reconciliation is no easy task, but Jonathan's unique style has brought out the human aspect in each story, which contains a trace of hope for the future. Through his eye for detail and his vivid depictions he demonstrates that all people are the same, we all share the same hopes and dreams, the same fears and anxieties, and the same God.

On a personal note, it has been an honor and a privilege to share a part of this journey with Jonathan, and I am extremely thankful for all the work, time, and effort he put into the realization of this dream. I would also like to thank Sara Fischer, Ambreen Tour Ben-Shmuel and Joshua Korn for their editorial work on these stories. Without their help this project would not have been possible. I hope that the stories in this volume will inspire, challenge, and motivate others in the way they have inspired, challenged, and motivated me.

SALIM J. MUNAYER
Musalaha Director

Preface

"**Y**OU HAVE heard it said . . . but I tell you . . ."
These are some of the most life-threatening, and life-giving,
words I've ever heard. They strip me of my securities, they rob
me of my comforts, they take away my preconceptions. They tear
down my strongly-held religious and political convictions. They
tell me to look, not higher, but deeper, toward the heart, toward my
heart, toward others' hearts, toward the heart of reality. They tell
me that deconstruction is an act of love. Jesus disturbs our settled
words because he tells us of a radical kind of God; radical in the
more common meaning of "revolutionary," but also in the Latin
origin which means "to the root."

These words tell me to look again. Without that respect, which
means "to look again" in Latin, we will not see.

I came to volunteer with Musalaha for six months, beginning
in September 2009 through the end of February 2010. Between
September and December, I conducted approximately thirty interviews with people, Israeli and Palestinian, who are involved with the
organization. I traveled from Jerusalem to Haifa, from Bethlehem
to Nazareth, meeting in coffee shops, offices, and homes, asking a
few questions to serve as a framework and allowing the conversation to evolve from there. For the next several months, I incarnated
my skeletal notes as stories about encounters with "the other" and
events of reconciliation. The project was not a comprehensive

biographical endeavor; I had only one interview with each person. Because of that, I am not completely satisfied with all the stories, which is inevitable when writing. Interviews in coffee shops and homes, divorced from action and interaction, provide a limited palette of descriptive hues. And this project was not an attempt to relate the history of the conflict. Much better and more educated people have dealt very extensively with that subject. These stories were meant to be small windows into the ongoing transformation of specific people.

Some stories are short, some are longer, and some are told together because the accounts were marked by a specific encounter with each other. In each story, I gave the last word to the main character. I certainly do not agree with or condone every perspective shared, but this book was not intended to explicitly counter each disconcerting point of view. These stories are an attempt at conversation, allowing different thoughts and opinions to unsettle and unhinge our own thoughts and opinions. To at least make us look again. Tensions are preserved and several of the endings seem abrupt because those tensions have not all been resolved. Transformation is a never-ending journey.

Not every reference to history or to current events is factual. Those interviewed were speaking from memory, without reference to verifiable sources. They, like all of us, speak out of their framing stories which provide legitimacy for why we think, feel, and act the way we do. We need framing stories. We cannot help having them, but we can help which ones we live out. We need a new one that speaks of justice, reconciliation, and peace. And the first step is to open ourselves to listening to the stories of others.

National defense strategies and political resolutions have never created space for this opening and listening. They cannot. Oppressive systems and extremist violence must be confronted, but if people are still tied to the destructive mindsets that engendered these violent systems, then little will be changed, and the brutal cycle will continue. Maybe one step to overcoming the oppressive political and societal systems is to dismantle the racial prejudices and uninformed worldviews held fearfully by so many people. To transform hearts. Many would say this is foolishly naïve. And it is. "But God chose the foolish things of the world to shame the wise; God chose the weak things of the world to shame the strong." Like Hercules fighting the Hydra monster, we can and must chop down the countless destructive systems forever, but they will always grow back like biting heads unless the people in the systems rethink everything. We can only ignore the source for so long.

I hold no illusions of being or wanting to be a politician, at least not in the typical sense. I have no grand theories or clever schemes that if implemented will end this turmoil. I want to be a storyteller; I have stories I want to tell because I foolishly believe in their transforming power. There will be no peace without conversion through reconciliation and justice. I do not mean justice characterized as "getting what you deserve," justice as the antecedent to "the American way," or justice as an "eye for an eye." The Holocaust cannot justify the *Nakba* and the Occupation; the *Nakba* does not justify suicide bombings and rockets. In the Jewish worldview, peace, *shalom*, is not the absence of difference or disagreement, but it is the presence of the wholeness of God. Justice is about rehumanization, because justice, as Dr. Cornel West says, "is what love looks like in public."[1] The Arabic word translated as "goodbye" is *maʾa salaama*, but a friend once told me that it literally means "with health," and comes from the same root as the word for "peace," *salaam*. Peace is healing, and healing brings wholeness. Justice is the arrival of that healing presence which washes away oppression and dehumanization and conquest; and mercy and compassion always flow within the mighty stream of true justice.

Frederick Buechner wrote that "In Hebrew the term *dabar* means both 'word' and 'deed.' Thus to say something is to do something . . . Words are power, essentially the power of creation. By my

1. Justin Dillon, Director, *Call + Response*, 2008.

words I both discover and create who I am. By my words I elicit a word from you. Through our converse we create each other."[2]

Words and actions create stories and stories create meaning. Stories say something and do something. May these stories create an open space for the sacred event of what seems like the impossible to happen, because stories not only describe reality, they transform it. They tell us to keep looking again.

JONATHAN MCRAY

2. Frederick Buechner, *Wishful Thinking: A Seeker's ABC*. San Francisco: Harper-One, 1993.

Contributors

Salim J. Munayer, former Academic Dean and lecturer at the Bethlehem Bible College, co-founder and director of Musalaha.

Lisa Loden, former director of the Caspari Center for Biblical and Jewish Studies in Jerusalem, member of Musalaha's advisory board, and lecturer in the Department of Leadership Development Studies at the Nazareth Evangelical Theological Seminary.

Munther Isaac, lecturer and assistant Academic Dean at the Bethlehem Bible College, currently pursing his Ph.D. at the Oxford Center for Mission Studies.

Philip D. Ben-Shmuel, currently working on a degree in Biblical Studies and Comparative Religions at the Hebrew University of Jerusalem.

Shireen Hilal, lecturer at the Bethlehem Bible College, Project Co-ordinator for Musalaha's Women's Department.

Evan Thomas

O NCE A month, Musalaha's staff and participants gather at the Talitha Qumi School in Beit Jala, northwest of Bethlehem for curriculum teaching. The German-operated school is the best location for such meetings: it's in the West Bank, so Palestinians can attend, but it's accessible by Israelis because the main road down the hill leads to settlements in Area C. Musalaha's curriculum teaching seminars deal with important topics related to the Israeli-Palestinian conflict, endeavoring to find the tense place for shared-faith reconciliation within that conflict.

In the middle of October, everyone gathered in a corner room on the top floor of the school's guesthouse. We sat around a wide table that filled up the center of the room and papers for note-taking were passed around the table's edge. Even in October, the heat in the room, fueled by large numbers crowded in a small space, was enough to make people squirm uncomfortably in their seats. The windows were opened and the cool air came in with a faint scent of pines from the courtyard.

Evan Thomas unbuttoned the top button of his short-sleeve shirt; the heat still lingered even with all the windows wide open. Evan, the Chairman of the Board of Musalaha, continued his presentation from the previous month of a study on Israeli Messianic Jewish identity, attempting to unpack the intricate layers involved in such a label. Beads of sweat dripped beneath the rim of his glasses, perched on the edge of his nose as he read slowly from a thick packet of papers. He used his hands frequently when he spoke, and his gestures were smooth, like sign language, inviting the listener to relax and become part of the conversation. And the listeners did join. Throughout his lecture, he was interrupted by enthusiastic affirmations and perplexed questions, and he would softly set the packet of papers down and lean forward toward the speaker. He seemed to have an incredible gift for making the other person in a conversation feel valued, like their opinion was really worth listening to. At times, the discussions turned into arguments and brows furrowed and words were sharpened, but Evan's large hands started moving and he gently interceded and quelled the rising storm. The man was a natural mediator.

After the lecture, everyone migrated downstairs to a buffet meal and sat in close huddles around long tables, consuming pita and consumed by conversations of identity. Evan and I moved to a circle of couches and chairs on the other side of the room from the tables. He tried to stifle a yawn and he scratched his buzzed hair, thinning near the back of his head. Aside from his role as Chairman of Musalaha's Board, Evan is also the Chairman of the National Evangelism Committee of Israel and is on the Board of Directors of the Israel College of the Bible. Not to mention that he is one of three pastoral elders for Beit Asaph, a Messianic congregation based in Netanya. Despite his busy schedule, he had excitedly agreed to meet with me and afterwards to take me to Jerusalem's central bus station; I would be spending the weekend hiking and camping around the Sea of Galilee with my housemates. His pleasant Kiwi accent easily gave away his country of origin. Herschel and Esther, his grandparents, were originally from Jerusalem, but left at the start of the twentieth century, settling down in the green hills and white mountains of New Zealand. In university, I spent a semester studying in Australia and hopped over to New Zealand, although all of my time was spent on the south island and Evan was from the north island. He was born in Whakatane, a fishing town on the Eastern Bay of Plenty, which, on a map, actually looks more North.

"I have a great love for the sea," he said with a smile, leaning back with his right arm stretched comfortably on the top of the couch. "The outdoors were a large part of my education. I still have a boat, a small boat, because my wife Maala's and my home in Netanya is very near the Mediterranean. It's only about a ten minute drive from our home."

The seat cushions suddenly began sliding out from under him, so he sat forward as we talked, thoughtfully rubbing his large hands together. Unfortunately, we had limited time together: Evan had to make his way west to Netanya and I needed to catch a bus to Tiberias. So, Evan provided a brief summary of his earlier years and conversion, but promised to send me a story he had written which detailed both at greater length.

Evan grew up in a secular Jewish home. His grandparents were deeply devoted to their religious faith and spoke with fervent longing for "the Land," but his parents decided to allow their children to make their own spiritual decisions, when they were older. And for the early part of his life, Evan was content, and he studied and married and began a career in his native New Zealand. But things began to change in 1977, two years after his marriage, when Evan was twenty-four years old.

Maala, now a teacher and guidance counselor, gave "her life to Yeshua (Jesus)." And, Evan says, a radical change occurred in their life together. In the story he sent me, Evan writes that "[s]uddenly I had an 'angel' for a wife." The tensions that had so far infused their marriage vanished, or at least were resolved more calmly.

"As a result," he writes, "rather than object to her faith I proceeded to encourage her, inviting a local Christian Pastor to teach a weekly Bible study in our home (which I didn't attend), insisting she regularly attend services, to which I would often take her."

But Evan didn't immediately follow in his wife's footsteps, and his enthusiasm for his wife's transformation grew from the absence of conflict and her newfound service-oriented heart.

"To this day I am ashamed of my selfishness."

3

Almost a year later, while Evan was studying at Massey University, he impulsively popped into a movie theater in order to escape his intense studies for a few hours. The film was *The Hiding Place*, based on Corrie Ten Boom's account of her family's life-threatening sacrifice to save Jews from the Nazis in Holland. As he sat in the darkness, Evan felt something changing, like his hardened heart was being kneaded and leavened by the story he encountered. His academic explorations of the Jewish and Christian Scriptures slowly became more personal "as I quietly gave my life to Yeshua and knew His forgiveness."

In the midst of familial concern, Evan's commitment to Yeshua caused him to return to his Jewish roots. And for him, as for many others, this newfound belief that Yeshua was the Messiah of the Jews, and the Gentiles, coincided with an instantaneous desire for "the Land." That faraway place of his grandparent's stories emerged in his thoughts. Then, one morning in 1979, he woke Maala up and dictated words that were running through his mind: "Prepare, for I will take you to the Land and there I will teach you much." Evan interpreted these biblical words as a direct message and he and Maala immediately packed their bags and set off for a kibbutz in Israel's Sharon Valley, where they worked for the next fourteen months.

"This period was to be the 'honeymoon' of our walk with the Lord and the formation of our relationship with Israel."

The plan was always to return to New Zealand, but Evan slowly began to feel differently, that perhaps Israel should be their home. Evan became convinced that "the ingathering of the Jewish people" to Israel was necessary. He and Maala returned to New Zealand in December of 1980 and began preparing for *aliyah*, their permanent immigration as Jews to the State of Israel. In 1983, they went back to Israel.

Evan and Maala came to Netyana; they had loved the Sharon Valley during their time on the kibbutz, and so decided to make the coastal city their home. The sea still called to Evan, even if it was a different one. For six months they studied Hebrew in their crammed apartment and attempted to integrate into their new culture. They found jobs and reconnected with a group of local Messianic Jews that they had known several years before. Evan was soon asked to serve as an elder and his desire to step more fully into ministry began to grow. After four years, he devoted himself full-time to the congregation of Beit Asaph, the House of the Convener. Begun in the 1970s by David and Lisa Loden (who is also on Musalaha's Board), Beit Asaph originated as a consolidation of two house groups, and this grassroots foundation, along with its encompassing name, has led to a more inclusive vision. Beit Asaph is comprised of more than two-hundred members from various ethnic backgrounds, including immigrants from Russia, Ethiopia, and South America. The congregation is also marked by a deep commitment to helping the severely disabled in their community.

Evan shifted as the seat cushions began to slide again. Two German volunteers were carrying the dirty dishes and empty food platters back to the kitchen. I turned the conversation to Palestinians.

"In first coming to Israel," Evan said, running both hands through his whitening beard, "I had little or no interaction with Palestinian Christians. And my interaction with Palestinian communities was with my military service in Gaza and areas of the West Bank, like Hebron, Qalqiliya, and Tulkarem. I was sent all over during the first *intifada* in the early 1980s."

He spoke slowly and carefully, choosing each word.

"My perception of Palestinians was as a soldier seeing them as a hostile environment to my own. I didn't have any personal enmity to Palestinians. It came as military-based, as a result of my training. I just saw them as an enemy to my own people. In a civilian setting I had no negative interactions. The word 'Palestinian' didn't come up at that point. Reconciliation, as far as I knew, was not discussed as an important issue in the believing communities."

Evan seemed unaware of a wider, deeper conflict between the two peoples until a large prayer conference, which included both Jewish and Palestinian Christians, in the mid-1980s.

"I don't remember much about the content, but I do remember the conference turned into a total debacle when Gazan Palestinian Christians began to hand out fliers, what about I don't recall, and that infuriated the Israelis and all was disbanded. My recollection is imperfect, but it seems to me now that the conflict with our larger communities was suppressed because people said we are one with Christ and that there is no conflict."

Apparently that wasn't entirely true.

Evan finished military training after his first four months in Israel in 1983, but reserve duty was required for the following fifteen years, and he was called up in 1987 when the first *intifada* broke out. In 1988, Evan was on combat duty in Gaza City. He was stationed at the entrance to the city and performed body searches on Palestinian men passing through the gates, most of whom were attempting to obtain permits to visit families in the West Bank.

"We had been trained not to look into the faces of the people we were searching," Evan said, holding his hand over his eyes, "so as not to become acquainted or familiar with anyone."

But one particular day, he did look up, and even though he had been taught that there weren't any faces to look at, he found the face of a young man looking back into his. And they recognized each other.

"From that conference!" Evan declared.

An Israeli soldier and a Palestinian recognizing one another in Gaza City made for an awkward situation, but Evan quickly realized that they were faced with a much larger dilemma.

"If my superior had seen me I would have been severely reprimanded, and for him to greet an Israeli soldier would not look good in the eyes of his people either. The interaction between us was a true example of facing your enemy as a brother. This was the same year, and not long before, Musalaha was forming and Salim approached me to help form this important ministry."

His large hands were folded in front of him and he looked at the tiled floor.

"This memory has stayed with me so vividly, that I believe, John, the Lord ordained it in order to soften my heart. But each successive tour of duty in the West Bank challenged me enormously, as did becoming aware of the pain of the second-class status of Palestinian citizens in Israel. Not so much my politics," he added rather quickly, "but my theology was sharpened."

I wasn't sure what he meant. Were his politics not changed because his presuppositions, whatever they were, were reinforced, or because his politics were not formed enough beforehand? He thought for a moment and affirmed the latter.

"I come from New Zealand, and politics there are just not that important. So at the time I was pretty much an open book. Most of my theology that developed as a result of my early training in New Zealand no longer seemed as relevant after two years of being here in the Land. I was, however, left with a deep relationship with Yeshua, a connection to the land, and wonderment in discovering my Jewish identity. As I said, my theology was sharpened in these tours, especially things such as 1 John 4, especially verse 20."

I couldn't remember the words offhand and had to look the verse up later: "If anyone says, 'I love God,' yet hates his brother, he is a liar. For anyone who does not love his brother, whom he has seen, cannot love God, whom he has not seen."

Evan took a class on biblical counseling and ministry skills among indigenous church leaders at a study center in Tel Aviv. There he met Salim Munayer, an energetic Israeli Palestinian from Lod who was both a student and director at the center. Through the intensive course, the two got to know one another intimately and discovered they shared an intense desire for reconciliation, for *musalaha* and *ritzui*, between Israelis and Palestinians. And visionary Salim's candid personality worked well with pastoral Evan's diplomatic nature.

"Salim shared with me one of those visions, about forming an organization that sought to bring about that reconciliation by first bringing together people from the Israeli community"—

and his right hand swept in like a broom—"and people from the Palestinian community"—and his left hand swept in and clasped with the other—"through the commonality of a shared faith."

This was certainly a huge undertaking. I wondered if he felt apprehensive at all, but Evan cut in before I finished the question.

"I had absolutely no hesitation, because I believe the Lord prepared my heart. I say that deliberately, not as superficial God-talk that so many use. I am too down-to-earth practical to get overly enthusiastic, as Salim always is, but I was never hesitant."

Not long after, Musalaha began to take shape, with Salim as the Director and a Board of Oversight equally divided between leaders from the Palestinian Christian and Messianic Jewish communities. This structure, which allows decisions to be made by both sides, has become a major element in Musalaha's endeavor for conversational equality. Evan was fully engaged since the beginning, helping develop the organizational infrastructure and participating in desert encounters. At first, the desert trips consisted only of young adults, Palestinians and Israelis.

"The first desert encounter in 1990 was highly successful, even with fifty people," Evan said. "The desert as a classroom was the great leveler."

Soon, the three-to-five day trips began to include well-established religious leaders, men and women, from both sides. As deeper and more challenging issues arose, the desert became a place where people learned to listen. The wilderness stripped everyone of their comforts and familiarity, creating the safe space where the stranger could be given a name and a story. And those that committed to the emptying process began to form intimate relationships with the people they once called "enemy." The desert was where possibility was present for dried bones to be filled with new breath.

Then Salim began to form a theology of reconciliation influenced by Eph 2:14–16: "For he himself is our peace, who has made the two one and has destroyed the barrier, the dividing wall of hostility . . . His purpose was to create in himself one new man out of the two, thus making peace, and in this one body to reconcile both of them to God through the cross, by which he put to death their hostility." Musalaha became recognized as an expert in reconciliation in some areas of the country, and the recognition spread overseas until study groups began coming to learn from Musalaha and to raise awareness of the fiery conflict. Evan and Salim began traveling and speaking together. After Israel and Jordan signed a peace treaty in 1994, the two brothers crossed the Jordan River to meet with Christian communities, many of which were Palestinian refugees. Evan and Salim still work closely together, communicating any time major decisions arise.

Evan looked at his watch and decided it was best to be on the move. We stuffed our papers in our bags and drove down the hill to the main road. We passed too easily through the checkpoint and drove into Jerusalem. We soon arrived in West Jerusalem, busy with traffic and pedestrians. We talked about other things, about the sea and about gardening, but before I exited the car I remarked that Beit Asaph certainly sounded like a very inclusive congregation. I wondered if Evan ever had problems with racism stemming from the conflict.

"Fortunately," he said, checking and adjusting his rearview mirror, "I have not had to confront overt racism toward Palestinians in my own community but I have had to confront racism in general. Some of the strongest was toward Germans or ethnic groups in my own community. Or between Jews and Gentiles. A lot of it was based in racist or elitist thinking. So the things I was learning in the field with Musalaha made me highly sensitized to such views and growing tools to confront it. Large numbers of my congregation have had interactions with Palestinians through Musalaha. Several of my colleagues have gone to be leaders in inter-community movements. There's no doubt that at times our positions, or rather agendas, have been viewed with some disdain and suspicion, both theologically and sociologically. But meeting with our Palestinian brothers and sisters is part of our basic vision. It is necessary."

Sarah Atwood

O N ALMOST every block of Hillel Street, thumping bass music emanated from cafés and bars into West Jerusalem. The music wasn't loud, crashing out of doorways and disrupting conversation and the late summer air. But the pavement resonated beneath my feet with techno beats. People entered and exited in clusters, funneling to and from Ben Yehuda, the city-center promenade. The sun was going down and the streetlights were coming on. This street in West Jerusalem felt like a European city.

I sat down on the steps in front of Café Aroma, and the name, at least for this particular one, was apt because I could smell the strong coffee. People sat in quiet conversation around circled tables on the patio. I wished I had brought a jacket as an unexpected breeze hit me, lingering, and people on the patio tugged on their collars. I was surprised by how cold it suddenly became and I crossed my goose-bumped arms, squeezing my chest with my elbows.

"Excuse me, are you John?" a voice said to my right.

I turned and looked at a girl with sunglasses pushing back her long brown hair. She introduced herself as Sarah Atwood, and she looked at me quizzically as I huddled over and shivered. Sarah apologized for being a little behind schedule, but work ended later than usual. Fortunately, she worked around the corner, as a secretary in a law office that mostly caters to Messianic Jews and

Christians, so walking to the café didn't take very long. I asked her where she wanted to sit. She thought for a moment as she put on a light sweater.

"Oh, let's sit outside," she said.

Sarah briefly disappeared inside to order a cup of something hot and I looked for my notebook in my backpack. For some reason, I didn't order any coffee. I would just try to keep warm from the steam issuing from my fast-moving pen. We sat at a table just outside the door. I faced toward the street and watched partygoers and businessmen hurrying past as I waited. Sarah soon returned carrying a bowl-sized cup of cappuccino topped with whipped cream, like a nebula swirled with a chocolate-powder galaxy. She pulled a half-empty carton of cigarettes from her pocket, sticking one in her mouth and flicking a lighter at one end. She seemed skeptical of me, almost uncomfortable with the whole idea of the interview.

Sarah was born in Israel and raised in a very orthodox Jewish household. Her dad made *aliyah* from New York, which was evident in the slight inflections of Sarah's English. Her mom immigrated to Israel from England.

"I was very sheltered," she said, waving her hands as she spoke. Her cigarette left blurry circular trails like overexposed photographs and ashes dropped onto the patio.

"What I knew of Palestinians is that our neighborhood was shot at and that the Wall runs near my parent's house. That was it."

But, in 2008, she was introduced to the teachings of an ancient Jewish carpenter whose way of life she began to believe was the fulfillment of Jewish law and prophets. She kept her new faith quiet for awhile, worried about her family's reactions. And with this new faith came questions about the people on the other side of that Wall near her parent's home. Maybe the teachings of this person she believed was the Messiah, who at every turn challenged the sexism, classism, and ethnocentrism of his day, had something to say about Palestinians.

"I met some Israelis Arabs after I became a Christian, including Nussi Khalil, and she does young adult work for Musalaha. She told me about the work that Musalaha does and invited me to come to Jordan on one of the desert experiences."

Sarah took a sip of her drink and tapped her second cigarette against an ashtray.

"I think I was very open to it, but I was definitely nervous. I didn't really know what I was getting into."

Four months after her entire life changed, she went to Wadi Rum with a group of Israelis and Palestinians. The trip was the first time in her life that she was on equal ground with people she once thought of as her enemies. Throughout the week she felt like a wind was crumbling her stereotypes in the face of friendship. Talking and listening and sharing emptied her so that she was ready to be filled with something new. One day, the group raced through the canyons in jeeps.

"Five or six people were placed in each car and, of course, at least one person next to you didn't share your ethnicity. You're very close to each other and you really have to listen to the other side in such a tight place. You can't really get away if you wanted to. The only thing you have to do is listen. I realized that they share the same kind of pain, but on the other side of the hallway I guess. And then, in the evenings, we were split up again, one Israeli and one Palestinian, and we had to sit down and pray with each other and again we found so much in common and dropped so many of our differences in the desert. It really showed how human we all are. We did the opposite of dehumanization really fast."

When she left for Jordan, her family still didn't know about the new facet to her faith. But her dad soon found out when pictures of her with Palestinians at Wadi Rum were posted on Facebook. Sarah was surprised that her family didn't react very negatively, but some of her more religious friends were very upset. But they were more upset because she now had friends who were Palestinian.

"I went to a very Zionist high school," she explained, "and during the second *intifada* there was a lot of very anti-Arab stuff going on in my school. I mean, when you're caught up in the midst of that, you find yourself going along with some things. I mean, people you knew were being killed and you kinda feel compelled to hate them."

Her face turned red, like she was ashamed, and she opened her mouth to say something, but stopped. She leaned forward, maybe trying to see what I was writing down in my notebook.

"I don't know if I can say that. But I have had a complete transformation in my passions."

Even though entering the West Bank is illegal for Israeli citizens, she once snuck into Bethlehem using her American passport. Sarah wanted to see what life on the other side of that Wall was like.

"They always say stones can talk," she said. "The Wall really tells a story that needs to be heard."

Not long after her desert trip, Musalaha sent out a mass email concerning a trip to Norway. They wanted to send an Israeli and a Palestinian to speak about the organization's work in schools, churches, and universities. She learned that the Israeli originally going had to pull out, so she volunteered. In February of 2009, Sarah went to Norway with a Palestinian guy from Bethlehem named Raed Hanania. The trip was a difficult one for both of them. Sarah was very frustrated by the more pro-Palestinian perspective she encountered in the universities; Raed was deeply hurt by the unquestioning support of Israel that confronted them in some of the churches.

"We felt like many of the people we met were very cold so Raed and I became good friends and I really realized how similar we were. We have to realize there are two sides, and for us to be together with a common faith, at least something in common, it was good."

I asked if she thought the conflict in this land would ever stop. After I asked, I wished I hadn't, because it's almost a ridiculous question without any possible answer. But she responded with a brief story.

On the plane back from Norway, she sat next to two Muslim teenagers. At one time in her life, she would have been afraid. But she remembered the cramped jeeps racing through the desert, which weren't all that different from a cramped jet flying through the air. She started talking to them and telling them about her trip to Norway. They were extremely interested in this Israeli who talked about Palestinians as brothers and sisters.

"It kinda gave me hope," she said, stabbing her last cigarette into the ashtray, pushing her mug away from her and her chair away from the table, "because here were Muslims who had a passion for peace and we could talk about it. All great things start small. So, I mean, what can one person do? We can do a lot."

Raed Hanania

R AED HANANIA stood in front of the sink. He thoroughly washed two mugs, glancing over at the kettle to see if the water was almost boiling. I sat in a swiveling chair next to his cluttered desk. His office combined a work space with a kitchen, and a large table seamlessly connected the two like a bridge. The kettle began steaming and Raed immediately flipped the boiler off and pitched two teabags into the sparkling clean mugs.

I met Raed two weeks earlier at the Talitha Qumi School in Beit Jala, where Musalaha holds a monthly curriculum teaching seminar. Evan Thomas presented the first of two lectures on Israeli Messianic Jewish identity before everyone gathered downstairs for lunch. Raed and I stood in line together and I soon realized that his name was on my list of thirty people to interview. He was incredibly friendly, constantly smiling, and he spoke quickly and laughed spiritedly. He had very short, curly, gelled hair, like almost every other Palestinian male his age. Between mouthfuls of pita and hummus, we talked about a possible upcoming interview and his impressions of Musalaha. I confessed that I had heard some questions concerning the organization and if, in all the vital and needed talk about reconciliation, talk about justice was ignored. He thought for a minute and looked around, his head lowering between his shoulders as we hovered over the table.

"Musalaha does many great things and I think it is so good to try and bring people from both sides together through, you know, a shared faith. But, sometimes, I think they try to say that we are equal, and we are not. In the eyes of God, yes, we are equal, but in the eyes of the people, the Israeli government, we are not equal. One side is occupying and oppressing the other and this we cannot forget. I believe we can live together, but we are not equal: we are under occupation. We are not both suffering in the same way."

Raed then told me about his job as the recently-appointed management deputy for Jemima, a home in Beit Jala for physically and mentally disabled children, and that he is now pursuing his second degree, a Masters in Organization Management and Development. He was excited when he learned that I was also working with the Al-Basma Center, which serves developmentally disabled youth in Beit Sahour. He immediately invited me to come and see Jemima. We soon jumped into his little car and he sped through the serpentine roads of Beit Jala, haphazardly shifting the gears without completely pushing down the clutch. He honked as we rounded every turn so that anyone on the other side knew we were coming, or maybe because everyone honks here, and everyone honks here constantly: people drive with one hand on the steering wheel and the other hand on the horn. Stoplights haven't changed from red to green before someone pounds the horn fifteen cars back.

Raed originally grew up in Bethlehem, raised in a nominal Greek Orthodox family. His two sisters and one brother are all married now, so he's the only one at home. He attended an all-Muslim government school, but he didn't really take his studies very seriously.

"We went to play, not to learn. And church was to meet girls. I graduated and I wanted to keep studying but I wasn't interested in anything."

At first Raed wanted to be a tour guide, but soon bumped up against the rigorous stipulations and procedures involved in acquiring a license. He jokingly said he settled for theology at Bethlehem Bible College (BBC). But then his expression became more pensive and he realized that he ultimately chose theology because he felt like he knew nothing about Jesus. At first, the courses were extremely overwhelming as he felt like everyone wanted to tell him everything in different ways. But during his third year his life changed. He believed that he could have his own relationship with God without a mediator. But he still didn't know how that relationship would be incarnated. He was still looking for the face of God.

And then Raed began working with Jemima while he was a student at the (BBC). He wanted to do something helpful even if he wouldn't be paid, something good because he said "Not doing something bad is not the same as doing something for God." Jemima needed volunteers and so the BBC put him to work there. A Dutch couple founded Jemima in 1982 and the place now consists of a small school and a living facility for the children. Jemima provides physical and speech therapy, and care-workers are on 24-hour shifts so that someone is always present. Mental disabilities in the Bethlehem area sometimes result from the close marriages common in Palestinian culture, and unfortunately a lack of awareness concerning disabilities devolves into stigmas and prejudices. A family abandoning their child because of disabilities is not unheard of. Some are left on the doorstep or in hospitals. Jemima welcomes the marginalized of the marginalized.

"I was always scared of handicapped people," he said with a shamed smile. "I would go to the other side of the street because I was afraid to walk past them."

"But my first job was a care-worker, so I was changing diapers, giving showers, and this, this changed me . . . it changed me a lot. I was touching them."

The Jemima complex cuts into the side of a steep hill, and as we pulled in on a small driveway between a playground and rock face, Raed said that Jemima was the name of one of Job's daughters. As we entered one of the living facilities, the children greeted Raed with enthusiastic shouts. He hugged them all and picked up a little boy with knobby knees and kissed his head. One of the little boys was three-years-old and still unable to talk. His head was almost as big as the rest of his body and very misshapen, like it had been squeezed in a vice. He couldn't focus his eyes to look at us and they kept rolling around. But he smiled. Another boy sat in a wheelchair. His legs were severely underdeveloped and his head was like an over-inflated balloon. His face couldn't fill up all the open space and so he tried to smile even wider.

Several weeks later, Raed poured the hot water into the mugs and stirred the seeping tea bags and brought one to me as I swiveled in the chair.

"Nice tea?" he asked expectantly. I scalded my tongue, but nodded and smiled through a bit lip.

"Really?" He was pleased, and hung his head sheepishly.

Raed sat down in his leather chair on the other side of the desk. He cautiously took a sip of his tea and strained the teabag before setting it on a napkin. He scratched his scruffy chin and leaned back in his chair, looking out of his office window beneath the top floor of Jemima. The tips of thin trees were visible over the window ledge.

"I had a story in my mind for a long time," he began slowly, and his eyes almost glazed over like his mind was time-traveling through memories. "I was playing with my brother and sister in Beit Sahour and my brother was fixing his bike and his hands were . . . um . . . you know"—his hands churned the air like he was propelling the words out of his mouth—"black, greasy I guess. This was during the first *intifada*. Anyway, we were in Beit Sahour and we started walking to my aunt's house, but before we got to the door an Israeli jeep stopped us."

The three kids continued walking, but the soldiers jumped out of the jeep and one soldier grabbed his brother by the shirt and yelled at him: "Why are you throwing stones at us? Look at your dirty hands! You have been throwing stones!"

"And they dragged him to the jeep and we were crying," Raed continued. "My sister got my family and my mother hurried to us and got on her knees and begged them not to take her son. But they pushed her down in the street. I hated a thing called Israeli soldiers, and this story was in my mind until I joined Musalaha in 2005."

Raed heard about Musalaha while studying at BBC. Salim Munayer was one of his professors and encouraged him to consider the desert encounter to Wadi Rum. However, Raed wasn't very interested in reconciliation, at least at first.

"I went more because my friends wanted to go on a trip. But this trip opened my mind because I realized I could be friends with Jewish people. In the desert we got to know people, sitting around fires and eating together, and I began to see that there are good people on the other side who are suffering."

But the unity Raed discovered in the desert began to disintegrate once he returned within the caged borders of the West Bank. The story of the soldiers and his brother with greasy hands haunted him once again. And he hated the thing called Israeli soldiers.

"Three big things in one week in 2008 made me feel *hallas*, enough, with Israelis and Musalaha," he said, shrugging them off with a flip of his hands. "My dignity was touched at these times, but I could do nothing."

Raed and a group of friends, including his Dutch ex-girl-friend, were on their way to spend a day at the Dead Sea and passed through one of the many Israeli checkpoints throughout the occupied West Bank. Raed ate from a bag of mixed nuts and watched as a soldier slowly marched around the car. Finally, the soldier stopped in front of Raed's door and ordered him to step outside. The soldier looked over Raed's ID and Raed, attempting to diffuse the sweltering tension, offered the soldier some of the nuts from the plastic bag. The soldier knocked them from Raed's hand, sending raisins and almonds flying to the dirt. And then he ordered Raed to take off his shirt and made him twist, holding his hands over his head. Raed was shaking with anger, boiling up inside until he almost exploded with the enraged humiliation in front of his girlfriend and his friends. Then the soldier tossed his shirt back at him and informed them that they must turn around because they could not pass through.

Several days later, Raed and a friend were driving to Ramallah. At the checkpoint, Raed was ordered from the car; a soldier standing at the vehicle's rear motioned for him. As Raed came closer the soldier lifted up the muzzle of his M-16 and pointed it at Raed, and told him to read the license plate number out loud. Raed laughed, saying the soldier could read it himself. The muzzle of the gun lifted higher and Raed slowly read the numbers. The soldier began making notes on a clipboard, then suddenly tossed the pen to the ground. He told Raed to pick it up. Raed refused. The gun was raised again. Raed lifted his hands and told the soldier to do it, shoot him. He was done with the humiliation. And Raed said the soldier could see the anger burning in fiery veins across his eyes and the soldier bent down and picked up the pen and moved on.

That same week, a Dutch family volunteering with Jemima asked Raed to show them around Hebron. He was reluctant, considering how the first part of the week had gone. But he decided to join them and gave them an unofficial tour through the agitated labyrinthine streets. Raed eventually brought them to the Tomb of the Patriarchs, the traditional resting place of Abraham and Sarah, Isaac and Rebecca, and Jacob and Leah. Part of the building is a mosque, and the other part is a synagogue. As they approached, one of the Israeli guards posted at the entrance began yelling at Raed, telling him he wasn't allowed to pass through with these foreigners. The Dutch family protested, explaining that Raed was their tour guide for the day, but the guards would not listen. There are lines for different people, they said, and Raed cannot pass through with them. It's a new rule, they explained. Of course it is, Raed responded, because you just made it up. So Raed waited while the family went inside. One of the young male guards asked him why he was traveling with these white foreigners, and then nodded toward the blond-haired daughter and asked, Have you gotten a piece of that?

"I said a lot of bad words about Israelis at that time," Raed said. "My picture was clear: they are my enemy."

He paused.

"A week later, I got an invitation to a Musalaha Desert Encounter," he said laughing.

He didn't want to go, and he struggled with the decision for several days. But soon he chose to give it another chance. The first day in the desert was interesting, but uneventful; Raed simply viewed the Israelis as foreigners and kept his distance as much as possible. He began watching people and noticed one guy, and Raed immediately knew he was a soldier. The way he walked and carried himself, the way his eyes surveyed the crowd. And as luck would have it, Raed was randomly put with him during the one-on-one session.

"His name was Mati Shoshani from Ma'ale Adummim. This is a very bad settlement. They have stolen so much water and land from Palestinians. When he started talking the first thing he said to me was that he was a soldier in Bethlehem for five years. He kept talking and I remembered all the bad things that soldiers have done to me. I got up and walked away."

Images of soldiers pushing his mother to the ground and muzzles of M-16s ordering him to read license plate numbers shot through his mind and the picture of his enemy became clearer and clearer.

But suddenly his hardened heart began to soften, and he wondered if this might be an opportunity for him to purge this hate, *hallas*, enough, and pray with this guy who looks and walks like a soldier. Raed ran to find Mati and sat down with him and began to unleash all the bitter stories and describe all the painful images.

"I told him everything, about the checkpoints, about the Dead Sea, about Hebron, about my brother when we were young. And he sat there and listened. He said he saw even worse things done to people, and he said he had quit the army because he cannot be in the army and be a believer at the same time, because they do not go together."

Raed spoke with bewilderment, like he was still processing the encounter, still being transformed by that event.

"And then he prayed for me, and we prayed together, and I thought: here is an Israeli who was in the army praying for me in the desert for the things the army had done to me."

Raed drained the last sip of tea from his mug and smiled, shaking his head. He put his hand over his heart and he looked me in the eyes.

"And this, this cleaned me."

Ros Khalil

Ros Khalil sat on the couch facing the television. She wore glasses and her hair was faded red, almost copper. She watched Al Jazeera with a bowl of fruit and sherbet. The commentators discussed Mahmoud Abbas' recent decision to postpone the Goldstone Report. Experts and reporters bickered in split-screens over the decision's efficacy.

"Oh goodness, that's about enough of that," she said, her accent refined and very British.

Ros set the bowl down on the coffee table. She leaned back into the couch. She began talking about Gaza, Obama, the difference between intentional and unintentional naiveté, healthcare. Her father, like mine, was a family doctor, "and what with national health in England we weren't very rich." The national system had its problems, she said, but a national healthcare system, at least theoretically, gave the poor just as equal an opportunity as the rich. And her father was able to retire after thirty years with pension.

"That was good terms, that."

I arrived in Nazareth earlier in the afternoon. My two roommates and I spent the weekend backpacking around the Sea of Galilee, hiking through holy sites and camping in isolated bays. On Sunday, my friends got a bus toward Jerusalem and I went west to Nazareth. Ros gave me directions over the phone, but the bus didn't follow the usual route and upon arrival, after walking a considerable distance in the wrong direction, I sat down on the roadside with a view of Mount Tabor in the valley. I couldn't find any street signs and, except for the lone conical hill in the distance, no distinguishable landmarks. Ros sent her husband George to look for me. Finally, after I mentioned a roundabout and some dilapidated warehouse across the street, Ros realized where I was and within fifteen minutes she drove up next to me as I waited by the curb.

The house was very quiet the following morning. Almost peacefully still. The Khalils have four children, but three have moved out. Their daughter Nussi coordinates Musalaha's young adult program. Marcus, the youngest, was at school. George was at work. The organization which he directs used to send out a Bible curriculum course by mail. During the second *intifada*, however, sending mail to the West Bank became almost impossible and everything was made electronic and available online. People throughout the world have now signed up for this course. The organization recently bought land to build a youth center with a library, cafeteria, and recreation area.

"There is very little for youth in Nazareth," Ros lamented. "It's rather ridiculous."

Soft white light scattered on the tile floor. Birds chirped in the tree just outside the double windows in the living room. Ros moved around the kitchen, opening the refrigerator and cupboards and emptying out containers. She insisted that we have a "light" breakfast: cereal, bread and jams, fruit, vegetables, and yogurt laid out on the counter between the kitchen and living area. And, of course, tea.

"I've been here thirty years and I still know how to make proper tea!" Ros exclaimed, setting a pot on the stove's grates.

After thirty years, she also speaks fluent Arabic, but reading is difficult and her Hebrew is spotty, which is more than I can say for myself in either language. Ros was mild-mannered, quiet and mostly unexpressive, but very friendly and open. Short bursts of bubbled laughter seasoned the conversation. She ate little, pecking small bits from different bowls and plates, her hands keeping warm around her mug. We talked about families and she said she grew up in a secular one in northwest London.

"Well, they were kind of churched, but my grandfather was a pastor and I think that turned my father off. Mother would take us to an Evangelical Anglican church and that's where I was saved."

During college, representatives from a Christian organization visited with pamphlets and pictures of remarkable places all over the world. Ros was immediately intrigued and did several summer trips to the Continent.

"After college, I felt the Lord was calling me to do a year of service," she said. "They had a major conference to introduce different fields and programs. I thought about doing a ship around Africa, but the ship was ghastly and four hundred people would be on it and I thought I'd go rather mad! Israel came up, so . . ."

She first came to the land between the river and the sea in 1976 in order to spend a year with a Christian organization doing literature distribution in Tel Aviv. At the time, she was much more supportive of Israel, even though she knew little of the history and current situation. She began to visit with people in Ramallah and Bethlehem and her eyes were slowly opened to a story she hadn't heard before. After her year was complete, she decided to stay longer and went to work in a Scottish hospice in Tiberias.

"Well, now it's the Scots Hotel and I can't recognize it anymore, all this five-star stuff they've put up over it," she muttered. "You know it I'm sure, down by the water? Well no matter. My college major had been Business and Tourism so I worked in reception and was very involved in all sorts of things, which was really exciting, because you certainly saw some weird people."

While working in Tiberias, she met George. Ros had friends at the Mission Hospital in Nazareth, and when she visited she attended his church. And to make a long story very short, she said, they were engaged in 1978 and married in 1979.

"My husband's family originally came from Jenin. His father was visiting Nazareth during '48 and the borders came down and he wasn't able to go back. He got married to a local girl and it took them years to get out of poverty. In the end they had eight or nine children. One was killed in an accident at a factory when he was fourteen. His hair got caught in the machine, and it scalped him, killing him. They received some sort of compensation and they were able to buy a small piece of land and build. Devastating."

She blinked several times and suddenly looked up at me.

"How did I get into all this?! Oh dear dear, you poor thing, just kept writing as I blabbered on about some other subject! Right, on to Musalaha!

"George was very bitter about what he had heard and seen. But then he met a Jewish believer named Art Goldberg and he showed no barriers to George. I think that was the change for him. Since age eleven, we put our kids in these Hebrew Messianic camps in Jerusalem so they wouldn't grow up entirely with that same bitterness. Sometimes they were the only Arabs there."

Their son Matthew recently married and is living in Iowa. Basil, the oldest, is a filmmaker and lives in London. Several years ago, he found a producer for his first big project. During one of the sieges of Ramallah, the Israeli military raided the production company and took all the money. The project collapsed. Basil and several of his friends planned to discuss their options at a restaurant over dinner, but at the last minute cancelled the reservation. A bomb exploded in the restaurant that evening. Basil was exasperated, packed up, and moved to England. I thought I saw Ros' eyes glisten at the edges, but she quickly wiped them. She supported her children, she said, but it was difficult to watch them moving off. She wanted her children to come home.

"Oh dear," she said. "There I go again. You came all this way to talk about Musalaha, and I talk about everything but."

Ros stacked a few dishes and placed them at the end of the counter. I tossed orange peels into my bowl where cereal flakes floated in a puddle of milk. She filled up our mugs with hot water and sat down again, elbows resting on the countertop and steam rising in front of her face.

"My first two-and-a-half years here I was mostly on the Jewish side, so I got to know them as people, but there weren't exactly all the tensions then as now. Or, at least I didn't know about them. My first impression of Musalaha was that they were only bringing together people who were already open to the idea of reconciliation, not the hardcore people. And there is some truth in that now."

Even so, she admired what Musalaha could do. But she felt uncertain of her place. She was married to an Israeli Palestinian, but she wasn't from here. Then she heard about Third-Side.

"I was having tea with this lady and she told me about this group Musalaha was starting for foreign ladies. That was about five years ago and we first met in a Catholic guest house outside of Jerusalem. Anyone who was at that first meeting will tell you it was incredible. Just really incredible. We all told our stories and they were all remarkable and different. We all had a very special bond. Everyone sort of sighed and thought 'This was the first place we've felt really comfortable.' Even if we had completely different stories, we had the same experience, all in the same boat sort of thing, both from the Jewish and Arab side: we all married into very different societies from our own, into an immense conflict. The stories of the other women were really comforting. Being here, adapting to culture, you go through some pretty hard times. And all of us could relate to see how others have tackled it. And some I thought, 'Wow, I thought I had a hard time!' You see other people's lives and how similar and different they can be. We used to, quite honestly, avoid deeper issues. But now the relationships are stronger because we go deeper. I rarely miss a meeting."

She closed her eyes, and her hands tightened around her mug.

"But there are some things on the Jewish side that still really make me boil," she said, her steady voice flustering with the pop of the last word. "There are processionals of settlers who want to require the British to apologize for what we did before 1948, but these settlers aren't apologizing to Palestinians for what they're doing to them now."

She laughed uncomfortably and shivered.

"I can't reconcile with that double-facedness really. I don't believe in apologizing for what you haven't done, and I do believe in apologizing for what you have done."

Ros sighed and set her mug on the counter. She looked at me for a moment, faintly shaking her head.

"This is why I love Third-Side," she said, now affirming with faint nods. "This double-facedness is talked about and exposed because we are sharing with one another. Even in our diversity we find support, because we are sharing a common experience as sort of strangers in another world."

At the last meeting, Ros told a story about family friends in Beit Sahour who, like many families, have not had water for five days. Their reserve tank is running low, because the irrigation systems favor the nearby settlements. The family once relied on an old well on their land when the water was shut off, but they returned home one day to find the Israeli military digging up the pipes and rerouting them toward the settlements.

"One of the women, married to an Israeli, was shocked. At first she couldn't believe it. She had never heard this before. But she wanted to understand. The dear thing was open. I suppose that's where we should all start."

Shoshi Danielson

I DON'T own a watch, so I looked at my phone. It was four-fifty, almost an hour after I was supposed to meet Shoshi Danielson. I had left the office in Talpiyot early, catching a bus to the Central Bus Station on Jaffa Street, and hopped on a *sherut* to Modi'in. Shoshi called and apologized for being so late and assured me that she was now on her way from nearby Na'ale; she had to wait until her husband returned home with the car. She directed me to the city center where I could wait for her at a small strip mall.

If I didn't know that Modi'in unevenly straddled the Green Line, I might think that it was just any other Israeli city, which is what most Israelis think. The city wasn't there fifteen years ago. The space was a Palestinian hilltop. Now, 70,000 people inhabit the growing metropolis. People jogged in tracksuits, kids kicked football in a field next to me, irritated drivers smashed their horns, and mothers pushed their strollers in tandem. Just like any other city. If I didn't already know, I wouldn't have any way of knowing.

Shoshi Danielson and her daughter pulled up at the intersection across from me, and Shoshi waved sheepishly through the car window. I climbed into the backseat and before I closed the door, Shoshi turned around and profusely apologized for being so late. She kept apologizing the entire way to a sprawling mall in downtown Modi'in. Her house recently burned down and the past few weeks had been incredibly hectic for her.

"My gardener was supposed to come last Wednesday," she explained. "But he came a week after and this made me late today and it's all just so bad!"

Shoshi parked the little car in the underground lot beneath the mall and the three of us entered the mall through an escalator. Teenagers huddled in amorphous blobs as they moved from music stores to clothes stores to electronic stores. Shoshi's daughter integrated into the blob with a group of friends. Shoshi asked me about my work and where I was from and where I was living now that I was in Israel. Actually, I told her, I don't live in Israel; I live in Beit Sahour.

"Oh, Beit Sahour! I know several women from Beit Sahour. Beautiful, beautiful people. But they don't speak much English, and so it's only '*Keyf halik?! Keyf halik?!*'"

She laughed and threw her arms around the air in a mock embrace.

Shoshi led me to a Café Joe's in one of the many corners of the enormous complex, away from buzzing conversations. The coffee shop had an expansive balcony and so we sat outside as the sun went down through the splattered clouds, like spilled orange juice. Shoshi ordered an ice coffee and I got a green tea. An orthodox Jewish mother sat adjacent to us, speaking to her baby in American English. Shoshi put her sweater on the sofa next to her and brushed her short hair from her face. She was incredibly amiable, and very genuinely open, earnestly leaning forward on her hands as she waited for questions.

"Well, I was born in Tel Aviv," she began, and added with a smile, "fifty years ago."

Shoshi was the firstborn in a secular Jewish family. Her mother was from Tel Aviv, and her father immigrated as a child from the border between Russia and Romania. Like all Israeli girls, Shoshi went to the military at eighteen for two years and was part of a unit that established a *kibbutz* by the Dead Sea. After Shoshi completed her military duty, she studied at Tel Aviv University. She read the New Testament for an art history class and somehow, she said, she just knew it was the truth.

While studying, Shoshi was not only discovering faith, but she was very politically involved.

"Very left-wing," she said, but her voice lowered to a hushed whisper. "I was very involved with the peace movement, so early on I had sympathy with the Palestinian's suffering very much."

She looked down and broodingly stirred her ice coffee with a straw, making widening fissures in the crushed ice. The sun was going down behind the outlines of apartment buildings.

"But I couldn't see the solution in the peace movement. I was very disappointed. I was disappointed in the people, who had nice high ideas, but everybody was in the same fight for power and status. I began to see that the right and the left eventually met on opposite ends."

Then she met Rolf from Sweden, who was studying art. They married and moved to his homeland.

"I was happy to move to Sweden and cut all ties with this complicated situation that I couldn't see the solution to. We moved to Sweden and we found God together."

The sun was gone now and the chill arrived. Shoshi put her sweater on over her black-and-white dress. The ice coffee probably wasn't helping.

"We moved to Sweden," she repeated, "but I always knew that we would come back."

She nodded slowly. She stared ahead, past the Jewish mother and her baby, and past the gray buildings. She seemed to be talking mostly to herself now.

"As a believer, I always understood that God wants his people here. I believe that God gave this land to the people of Israel. But when I left I was fed up with Israel and my people, and when I became a believer my views did not make sense with the word of God, with the Bible. I was fed up with what my people were doing, but this didn't make sense with God's plan for the people of Israel.

So I had to pray and ask God to change my views, to bring me back to his plan for this land."

In 1991, the Danielsons moved back to Israel and settled in Na'ale, what she called a "so-called settlement." They go to Sweden to visit occasionally, but as the years pass her husband wants to visit more often.

"When we first came back to Israel," she said, changing the subject and rubbing her hands, "I heard about Musalaha and thought it was very interesting. Lisa Loden asked me to be involved with women's activities. It fit with what I felt inside. But at the beginning I didn't interact with the Palestinians as much. This was as a result of the conference structure, which didn't involve a lot of personal interaction. We went to a family conference and it was very uncomfortable. We felt the Palestinians were trying to make us feel guilt for all their suffering, but we can't accept the blame. Why should we be blamed? We live in a sinful world and we all suffer from unrighteousness. We felt there was an expectancy that we should personally accept the responsibility which we can't. Because we felt so uncomfortable we stopped coming."

"I'm freezing with this ice coffee!" she blurted out through chattering teeth. We picked up our cups and moved inside. The long, thin room was sparsely populated and lamps cast dim patterns like Chinese fans on the wall. Even though we were now inside, Shoshi put her hands between her thighs to keep them warm. She picked up the conversation immediately.

"But some years ago I was asked to be involved with another women's group. And it was small and intimate. We went to Petra and became very close, ten women from each side. The women's activities are different because most of the women are not political, so the issues don't come up as often."

But the issues did come up in relationships, because there is no avoiding them. During the summer of 2006, on the first day of Israel's war with Hezbollah, the son of one of Shoshi's best friends was killed. Musalaha had a women's meeting scheduled on what would be the last day of the war, but Shoshi was afraid to go.

"I felt all my wounds would still be bleeding, and I was afraid that the Palestinian women would justify Hezbollah. And when I came there, everyone was so loving, everyone so accepting. I've learned more to identify with their pain, and I think they've learned to identify with my pain.

"I see peace possible only on the basis of our faith as a common ground. I cannot see any other solution that would bring peace to this place. This is the only common wings that we are under. It must be through faith. The women who are there will encourage their children, though my children have not been involved with Musalaha, unfortunately. But I think I gave them good education when it comes to that matter."

I asked if any of her Palestinian friends ever questioned the fact that Shoshi lives in a settlement.

"I was very interested about reactions to settlements, but it never came up," she said, her voice rising slightly in pitch. She was as genuinely surprised as I was. "I think it's amazing it didn't. One of my Palestinian friends from Musalaha came with me to this café, actually, and to my house, and she came to give me a present. She's very aware of where I live because her parents only live ten kilometers away. Even though they don't agree with the political implications, I think it's good for them to see that not all settlers have horns, that most of us are regular people who want to live in peace.

"I'm not here because of ideology, although I do believe that the settlements should be a part of this land. So I think it's good for them to see that so-called settlers are just normal people."

Even though the women's conferences are not very political, Shoshi said, some of them focused on topics like listening and identity.

"It's very hard, you know. We speak Hebrew, they speak Arabic and we don't always understand enough English, so how could we communicate? But this was the only chance for me to get to know the girls from the other side. Last year we discussed the *Nakba* and the Holocaust, and this was so hard, really, really hard. I was very distressed and I woke up in the middle of the nights, praying to God because I couldn't see how we could have the same Bible and then have such different views. But the most important thing is that we are brothers and sisters in Christ."

What did she mean: different views on the Bible? Shoshi didn't hesitate with an answer.

"The whole thing with God's plan for the people of Israel and the land. When I read my Bible, it's very, very obvious to me that this land is for the people of Israel."

She stopped looking pensively in the distance and looked me in the eye.

"I love my neighbors and I love the other people, but for me I don't see how you read the Bible and miss this point."

Shoshi suddenly stopped; her theological view clashed with theirs. She was quiet for some time, tracing the red straw around the lip of the empty glass. She didn't seem to know where to go or what to say next.

"But," she began almost inaudibly, dragging the word out until it hummed, "I don't know how this fact fits in here now, into this conflict. I don't have a solution. But to me it's very clear that God gave this land to the people of Israel. I don't know how this works politically."

Tamar Burdekin *and* Shadia Qubti

"I'LL JUST make some Bedouin chai," Tamar Burdekin called, peeking around the kitchen doorframe.

I sat in an armchair on the other side of the apartment. Toys were tossed in labyrinthine mazes on the floor. The wall behind me spilled over with books, and as I waited I perused the titles. The first thing I usually do when I enter someone's home is look at their bookshelves. I have a terrible habit of judging people by their book covers. Fortunately, I was prevented from temptation: most of the books were in Hebrew.

Tamar joined me before I could find many English titles. She carried a tray with honey cakes and steaming cups leaving slowly dissipating trails through the living room. English book titles wouldn't have helped my evaluation: this wasn't Tamar's apartment in Pisgat Ze'ev. She was staying with her sister, who was watching the kids up the spiraling black staircase near the front door, while she was in between houses and her British husband and brother-in-law were in the States building a house for her sister's family. Tamar told me she met her husband at a young adults group at the King of Kings congregation.

"You know, it's Zionist. Some of the sermons were quite political when I attended. In some cases I tried to argue but it was really futile. So, I met my husband there, but he was never so politically right-wing. He's almost more left-wing than me. Not too long ago, he was accosted by the Women in Green at a checkpoint on a back road into Beit Sahour. He goes to help with a climbing wall they have there. As he was going to a Palestinian village a woman started yelling at him hatefully, one even tried to get in his car! The army had to hurry and wave him through."

Subdued sunlight wove through the laced curtains and I could hear quick, repetitive footsteps above the ceiling as short legs raced across the upstairs floor. Tamar tucked her long skirt beneath her as she curled up on the couch. Her parents made *aliyah* from the United States, and Tamar was born in Israel. I told her that some of my friends informed me that a consensus has never been reached concerning the appropriate term for Jews who believed Jesus was the Messiah: should we say Messianic Jews, or Jewish Christians, or Christian Jews?

"Well, I was raised in a believing family, and went to a Baptist church for some time while I was growing up. I prefer to be called a Christian. Although, I guess being Jewish and going to church makes me a Messianic Jew. We went to a Messianic congregation when we were living in the States and they didn't have anything good to say about the Arabs. But, they aren't a part of the conflict, so I suppose their opinion on the matter doesn't hold much weight."

Tamar stared through the window as she talked, holding her mug with both hands in the folds of her dress. She was reserved, but friendly. She told me she worked as a secretary for Musalaha several years ago and is still involved in the women's group. She was first introduced to the organization over ten years ago by a friend, who invited Tamar and her sister on a desert excursion.

"My interactions with Palestinians before that were pretty much zero," she said.

"Well," she interrupted herself, "at summer camp growing up I guess there was an Israeli Arab girl. Growing up on the Israeli side, the common feelings toward Palestinians were fear and hatred."

She broke her gaze from the window and looked down into her cup. She laughed, almost an ironic laugh.

"It all seemed a little irrelevant because I didn't even know any Arabs! I always felt it was wrong to be prejudiced."

But even though Tamar knew racism was immoral, she was hesitant about joining Musalaha in the desert, a journey which led south to Eilat, across the border to Jordan, and north to Wadi Rum.

"There was a lot of uncertainty involved before going. I was very nervous. We didn't even know the Jews who were going. I turned twenty on the trip. I remember one Palestinian girl on the bus tried to be funny, but there was this whole language barrier and what she said didn't translate well, so we didn't get the joke and it was a little awkward."

She laughed again and put her hand over her forehead.

"It's a long ride to Eilat."

The first day of the trip was more awkward than the joke, she said, not because of any conflict, but because no one knew in which language to approach people. Israelis were naturally drawn toward one another, and Palestinians naturally pulled back into their own group. But the activities began to draw and pull everyone out of their ethnicity and into the larger group.

"The five days in the desert opened up communication. Just small, kinda like introductions and stuff. We paired up in the evenings to tell about ourselves and slowly, slowly we started knowing each other. Some girls started playing cards and, let me tell you, I love to play cards."

On the way back to Eilat, everyone spent a night in Aqaba. The forced interactions and teachings earlier in the week now provided space in which people were free to have fun, swimming and snorkeling. Friendships formed now that the wall, whether it was hostility or awkwardness, had been breached. And one special friendship formed for Tamar.

"I met this Israeli Arab girl named Shadia Qubti, from Nazareth. She was my age, and she knew English and Hebrew fluently, because she's an Israeli citizen. And we stayed up late and went out by the pool of the hotel, talking after everyone went to bed.

"And I just realized that she's not all that different from me. We exchanged emails and said 'Let's keep in touch!' Sometimes that doesn't end up happening, but we really meant it."

There were a few visits to Nazareth for Tamar and from Nazareth for Shadia and the friendship cemented itself. The other girls they befriended on the trip went back to their lives, but Shadia and Tamar continued to bond.

"Our relationship was a learning experience because I didn't know anything about Palestinians. Shadia told me a little about their history, like the *Nakba*, you know what that is, and their view of Israel, those Palestinians who are actually living in Israel. In Israeli schools we were told the very patriotic version and everyone is happy that yay, we get a country! We call it independence and they call it *Nakba*, you know, catastrophe. So, yeah, the different historical narrative was very eye-opening."

Tamar took my empty cup and hers into the kitchen. I heard a quick rush of water from the faucet and clinking as the cups fell into the sink. She called up the stairs as she walked past, making sure the children hadn't hurt each other. She sank back onto the couch. She seemed tired, or maybe sad, or maybe just missing her absent husband.

"I came back from that trip and was very, very left-wing, you know, questioning Israel and supporting Palestinian rights. My parents are very right-wing. I mean, they came here because they believe God wanted the Jews to be here. Eventually we just stopped talking about it. But I guess I've become more moderate since then. I think I belong in Israel."

She stared out the window again and her eyes squinted, but not from sunlight. A cloud hovered over the neighborhood and the dim light was now muted into gray. Tamar seemed uncomfortable, perhaps wrestling with complexities that remained irreducible in her mind. She blinked several times as she realized she was staring, and cleared her throat as she shifted back toward the middle of the room.

"I tried to be more neutral, but there is no neutral. I decided that it's not about being neutral, but it's about trying to see it through Jesus' eyes."

Uncertain, she added, "I guess."

Shadia Qubti sat in the shadows of a coffee shop above Mary's Well in Nazareth. The entrance led to a landing, which led down to tables and booths in corners. Besides us, only a few people populated the quiet restaurant. Artificial lights were turned off, and the room was illuminated naturally. Shade and light on the table were shaped in the form of the window frame, and Shadia traced the outline with her forefinger as we waited for drinks. The light highlighted her multi-colored bead necklace, but her nose ring was almost imperceptible as she leaned away from the window-shaped beam. Her dark, curly hair was gathered back in a ponytail and she wore glasses. She was strong, or rather confident, like a person who understands her limitations and abilities, and accepts them.

Shadia grew up in a Baptist family in Nazareth, the youngest of six children. Her mother was raised in an orphanage, along with other victims of the 1948 war. She and Shadia's father met through the orphanage. Her father taught at the Baptist school, which Shadia and her siblings attended their entire lives. Shadia was always interested in math and physics, and was very active in the student body, even elected part of the high school board. She had to be so involved, she said, because there wasn't really much to do in Nazareth, except hanging out with friends. They would go to movies or the mall in Nazareth Illit, the richer, and Jewish, part of town. Shadia grew up speaking three languages, one brother married a Northern Irish girl and another brother married a Swede, and she has a Jewish aunt, not through blood, but from her mother's orphanage.

"We're pretty multi-cultural," she said with a quick flashing grin.

She spent a lot of time at her aunt's home in Rehovot, near Tel Aviv, which is how she learned English. If she and her siblings spoke Arabic in her aunt's neighborhood, it was very hushed.

"Now, looking back, there were a few incidents," she said, leaning back sharply with one arm propped on the table. "I remember going up a slide at a playground, and we were speaking Arabic, and some girl stuck her tongue out at us and said something like 'Stinky Arabs!'"

Shadia rolled her eyes and added, "I probably stuck my tongue back out at her."

Once, when she was a teenager, her family vacationed in Eilat. She and her cousin snorkeled at the beach and he swam out further than Shadia. A few Israelis, some guys flirting with a girl, drifted between them. Shadia's cousin yelled for her to toss him the snorkel, but when Shadia threw it, the wind flipped it into the Israeli girl's face.

"One of the Israeli guys was really ticked off," she said, resting her chin on interlaced fingers. "I knew if I spoke Hebrew with my heavy Arabic accent, I was going to be ridiculed and used as a tool for him to impress the girl, so I spoke in English instead, pretending to be an American tourist. He really liked America, as do most Israeli Jews, so everything was fine after that."

Several years later, Shadia studied mechanical engineering at the Technion in Haifa.

"I was sitting in the cafeteria after some bombings occurred and this Jewish guy was talking about killing Arabs. I kinda shrunk inside because I didn't want to be anybody's punching bag. My fifteen-year-old cousin, just a few weeks ago, was grabbed by the police and they beat him up. They were looking for kids who were throwing stones, and he was running and they arrested him and beat him and only contacted his parents an hour-and-a-half later. Israel claims to be democratic."

She rolled her eyes again and shook her head.

"And there's an attitude that, in a way, just accepts all this. Palestinians get their IDs ready even before they get to the checkpoint. Why do this? I just wait until they ask for it. I shouldn't have to get it out because I'm Arab. Just because Israeli society sees me as secondary doesn't mean I have to give into their mold. Discrimination is very apparent, but still there is too much self-discrimination, victimization, accepting the place you are given.

"I feel like I've managed to accomplish a lot despite the discrimination and systemic injustice. And also because I'm Christian and not Muslim. This really perpetuates identity issues for people. Man, everyone has identity issues here! I mean, I'm a Palestinian, but I have Israeli citizenship. But I'm Christian, not Muslim. You just keep adding layers on layers and you really have no idea who you are. I was a teenager in the 90s, with the failure of Oslo and suicide bombings, and all these people shouting 'Death to Arabs!' and I wanted to be accepted. So I rejected the Palestinian in me. You can play with your identity here, especially as an Israeli Palestinian Christian. I was unsure of who I was."

Nazareth is the largest Palestinian city in Israel. Every year, the municipality holds a general strike, called Land Day, to commemorate and mourn past and ongoing land confiscation. And almost every year, the Israeli police interfere, kids throw stones, and the police chase them. Typical, she said, every year.

"My idea of Israelis was 'the police out to get you.' They'd catch the kids and beat them sometimes, but I never associated them with my Jewish aunt. I felt like there was some difference. Until the 80s, when Israel started recognizing the PLO, it was illegal to fly Palestinians flags and stuff, be publicly nationalist in any way, so growing up we didn't know that much about our own history. We studied Israeli history in school. But I started reading about the *Nakba* and watched a documentary about a massacre in 1956 and I started thinking more. And I struggled between these things, like being politically active, and church, because growing up these things were always pretty separate. Hating took too much out of me, and I didn't know how to do both at the same time."

So she decided not to hate. But she couldn't ignore this deep yearning to see change, a sense that maybe political involvement and religious conviction are not mutually exclusive. She told me that much of this path started on her first trip with Musalaha when she was nineteen. She didn't know anything about Messianic Jews and was surprised by the relationships she saw forming. Especially one relationship, on the last night, with a girl named Tamar. They spoke in English and Hebrew. But they didn't talk about abstract political theories; they talked about their own concrete experiences. Shadia was intrigued by Tamar's army experience. For Shadia, the army was an oppressing bully and all soldiers enjoyed harassment and discrimination. But Tamar hated her military duty, this forced duty to the state and being ingrained with hate for Palestinians.

"She helped me see that a lot of soldiers are kids," Shadia said as if the realization was still setting in, "these scared kids. Tamar's confidence in who she was, as a Jew, Messianic, whatever"—she flashed a grin again—"made me look more closely at my own identity."

Two years after they met, the second *intifada* erupted. The Israeli police came into Nazareth with more force than anything they had seen on Land Day. Snipers watched from the rooftops and jeeps patrolled the narrow streets. Shadia wrote mass emails describing the events in her hometown. She pointed out the window of the café to the square around Mary's Well, and said she remembers a demonstrator who was shot by snipers with rubber-coated steel bullets. Her uncle was shot with a rubber bullet as he was climbing to his roof. Luckily, his arm was over his chest. Tamar received all of these emails.

"What I told Tamar really contrasted with what she saw on the television, like one soldier was hurt and no mention of how many Arabs were injured. Her parents live in Israel, not because it's a good country or anything, but for ideological religious reasons, and they didn't accept what I said. I don't think they were calling me a liar or anything like that, but what I said just didn't mesh with what they needed to believe in order to live here. I think some things clicked for Tamar and she realized something wasn't right. We challenged one another. I think Musalaha works in this way. You can't really pinpoint it, but you know when it happens."

Shadia worked as project director for Musalaha for several years, but knew she needed more training in the fields of peace and conflict resolution. Then, she was offered a scholarship to go to Trinity College in Dublin to pursue a Masters in Peace Studies and Conflict Resolution. She focused all of her research papers, including her final thesis, on Israel and Palestine. Her intensive historical research and social analysis allowed her to finally reveal the full story of her people. The advent of this knowledge triggered a new confidence as the ethnic pieces of her identity started falling into place. And for the first time she began to embrace her heritage and accept all the parts of herself, Christian, Palestinian, Israeli citizen.

During the year in Dublin, Shadia took a break from church in order to surface from what she called "the oversaturation of Musalaha and other religious communities." She met people who were absolutely committed to justice and human rights even without religious beliefs. Through getting to know the (ir)religious other, in conversations about faith and life and through studying the history of her people, she began to know herself more.

"I began to realize that faith has been a positive impact, for me at least, shaping the way I see things. I won't deny there are some Christians who live in their spiritual bubbles and pretend like the world isn't there. But my conviction is different: we're supposed to be salt of the world."

"But," she quickly added, "if you put too much salt on something, it ruins it."

Shadia doesn't believe change is coming anytime soon. The imbalance of media coverage, and therefore power, is tipped too strongly in Israel's favor. But she never considered staying in Ireland.

"I knew I was coming back," she said emphatically. "I missed home very fast. The big question was what am I going to do when I come back? How was I going to put all this theory into practice? I left Jerusalem to study and I wanted to be in Nazareth, my community, to give back. The details are not clear at the moment, but I want to stay in the area of peace and reconciliation. Especially since

October 2000, this is filling in the gaps of my identity. Now I just need to mobilize all that I know. I definitely think the Palestinians in Israel have a big role to play in the conflict. The challenge is to figure out how to mobilize that, how to figure that out. We know both cultures, we speak both languages. The key is to be a bridge. That can be our identity."

Rittie Katz

I HURRIED off the Egged bus in Mevesseret Ziyon. Thirty minutes earlier, the bus left outside of the Jerusalem Central Bus Station and veered west out of the city into the coned hills, prickly with firs and pines. After only a few minutes, the bus turned right off the highway and slipped down and then up over the top of one of the hills. I was surprised by how quickly we arrived in Mevesseret Ziyon; and I was again surprised by how close everything in this country actually is. I had never been there before and didn't know where I was going. I sat on the edge of my seat, nervous that I would end up lost before I had any idea where I was. But as the bus prepared to leave, I noticed Café Joe out of the corner of my eye. I breathed a sigh of relief and disembarked, then realizing that I was over an hour early for my meeting with Rittie Katz, a member of Musalaha's Board. I sat on a park bench across the street from the café and finished a book by Walter Wink before jaywalking and waiting outside on the patio.

Five minutes later, Rittie burst around the corner. Her dark hair flamed out around her proud oval face and she wore reading glasses on a chain around her neck. I stood to greet her and she took my hand firmly and looked me in the eyes before sitting down. She was extremely jovial and forthcoming, but there was something quietly intense about her as she spoke in a New York accent. Her words were purposefully straightforward, and she spoke them in hushed tones; not necessarily because she was afraid of eavesdroppers, but because she was focused on this particular situation and the person involved. Rittie didn't talk about anything related to the interview until she had become sufficiently acquainted with me: where I was from, what my degree was in, how I ended up in this part of the world, and where I saw myself going. It seemed to me that Rittie wasn't so much interested in this meeting as a strict interview with some detached journalist; she wanted this to be a friendly conversation with another person.

The waitress stood next to Rittie as she held up her reading glasses and swept over the menu, mostly as a preliminary courtesy, before ordering in English. Even after eighteen years, she said, her Hebrew still isn't what it should be.

Rittie grew up in a very secular Reform Jewish family with little interest in God or in Israel. But her parents were deeply committed to human rights. Rittie was raised to favor the underdog, and after moving to the Middle East she knew she wanted, and needed, to be different here.

"Right away I knew we needed to reach out our hands to the Palestinians. I wanted to be part of the solution, not the problem."

During university, Rittie began looking into various religions and philosophies, including her own religious heritage. And then she watched Franco Zeffirelli's *Jesus of Nazareth* and for some reason was captivated by the performance and by the story, so rooted in her ancient tradition.

"Something about this man drew me closer in, something about his eyes, the way they saw you."

Rittie's voice lowered and she held up her hand, her fingers closing to form a circle. And then she laughed.

"And I thought I was going crazy, I was a psychology major!"

The waitress returned shortly with her cappuccino or mocha or something like that and my orange juice. Rittie sipped her coffee delicately so it wouldn't smear her light lipstick. Behind us, a group of construction workers loudly drilled the pavement near the front door of the café. Every time the drill started, machine-gun echoes pounding through the concrete, Rittie sat up and winced, closing her eyes in frustration.

Rittie and her husband immigrated to Israel eighteen years ago with a three-year old, fifteen month old, and pregnant with a third; a fourth came later. Soon after immigrating here, she took her young children to a park near their house. A lone Arab man was sitting on a bench near the swing set, holding a broom. She didn't say anything because she didn't speak Arabic and her Hebrew was mostly nonexistent. Before she arrived in Israel, she had resolved to reach out her hand to the underdogs she was raised to favor; but when the moment came, she thought of all the Western stereotypes and news images and she was frightened. She gathered her kids and stood up to go home.

But then she stopped.

"And I said to myself 'I am not living in fear' and so I sat down right next to him and said 'Hi!' I'm sure that was quite a shock, this Jewish woman trying to publicly talk to him, in English!"

But he was friendly, incredibly friendly, and didn't seem perturbed by her amiability. They began talking and she learned he was nineteen and had recently dropped out of school because of the first *intifada* to help his family with the little he earned by sweeping streets.

"Here I had all these things in my head from the media and they turned out not to be true," Rittie said. "At all."

Rittie came back regularly to the park with her children and her new friend always greeted them and picked up her kids and washed off their feet with a hose before setting them back in their strollers. Through the years, he has come to bar mitzvahs and other celebrations and, eighteen years later, is still a close family friend.

Salim Munayer became another close friend of the family, and all her kids were raised together with the Munayer's children. When her son Rafi was in fourth-grade, the teacher ("this so-called educator" she blurted out furiously) condemned Palestinians to the class. They were the enemies, she explained. Rafi raised his hand and said his best friend was a Palestinian. The classroom was quiet and the teacher, when her composure was regained, told him to be careful of the Arabs. Rafi said he should be more careful of the teacher.

Rittie heard Salim's passion and the vision he had for Musalaha and she knew she wanted to be involved somehow. She became part of one of the first small groups. She was amazed by the common ground she found through a shared faith, a continually recurring theme.

"I made a heart connection with a Palestinian woman named Salwa," Rittie said of a woman she had met at a Musalaha women's meeting, now speaking loudly over the incessant drilling. Sparks flew behind her and, from my angle, looked like they would catch her hair on fire.

"Salwa is like those people in *Star Trek*," she said expectantly, but my blank stare tipped her off to my ignorance. "Well, there are these characters, you know, that can take on the pain of other people."

At the time I had never watched much *Star Trek*, but not long after the interview, the disc drive on my computer sputtered and died, and my roommates and I began watching episodes of *Star Trek* one of them had copied on his new driveless computer. Her comment made sense weeks later.

"Anyway, she suffered with her people and I suffered with her. This conflict is much like a conceptual drawing, you know, the ones of a figure that could either be an old woman or a rabbit or something like that. Both perceptions are there and I understood that through Salwa."

Rittie now teaches special education in a mostly-Muslim school in Beit Hanina, a Palestinian neighborhood north of Jerusalem.

"I wanted to speak to the desires in my heart and it makes a statement for me to be there, like putting feet to my prayers," she said. "I certainly don't expect to change the world in Beit Hanina, but maybe I can till the soil and plant a few seeds."

Her job has not been easy. She is often faced with anti-Semitic remarks and vitriolic comments that consider all Israelis as one amalgamated entity. One of her students frequently talked to her about politics. His father is an ardent supporter of Hamas and the student began condemning Jews, detailing all the problems they have caused and will continue to cause. He reminded Rittie of Rafi's teacher. Rittie would sit across the desk from him, quiet and unsure of what to say. His visits continued, and his rhetoric intensified and finally Rittie said:

"You know, I am Jewish."

The boy fell back in his chair, his mind now rewinding through his many speeches. He paused briefly, and then slowly presented his litmus test: he asked her what she thought about "this so-called war" in Gaza. Rittie did not hesitate: the killing was despicable and her heart ached for the suffering people in Gaza. The boy saw Jews differently after that conversation. At least, this one Jew.

"I remember when the fighting in Gaza started," she said. "I came home one day and heard a neighbor screaming and wailing because her nephew, a soldier, had been killed in Gaza. Some of my friends had children who were stationed there as well. And I suffered with them too. I questioned whether or not to come to school the next day. I wasn't sure I wanted to be confronted by the stories and I was perhaps afraid of the possible attitudes toward me."

Rittie shook her head now as she spoke to me and lifted her chin.

"But I realized, like I did at the playground eighteen years ago, that I would not live in fear. So, I decided to come to school."

When Rittie walked through the doors, one of the Muslim teachers saw her and gasped, running toward her and throwing her arms around Rittie exclaiming "You came!" But other interactions were more difficult. She overheard students telling stories of families devastated by the Israeli attacks, and she heard students desiring to react violently against the soldiers.

"I had to understand that," she said, and tears began to peek around the corners of her eyes. She quickly wiped them away and cleared her throat. "For me, it's very simple. I don't have all these philosophical or theological things, explanations for everything I do. But, I know that to understand the other side is the heart of God and that has to be my heart."

One of the Musalaha women's conferences was devoted to this, she said. A Holocaust survivor and a *Nakba* refugee spoke together, telling their stories of persecution and loss and how they refused to hate their persecutors and instead chose a way of forgiveness. Rittie was in awe of the survivor and the refugee.

"I have tried to reconcile," she admitted. "Sometimes there doesn't seem to be anywhere to go. Where do we go from here when we are faced with challenging situations when each side suffers and each side is consumed with their own pain?"

Rittie leaned forward and her dark hair flamed about her head, and her forefinger and thumb pressed emphatically together.

"But I do believe Israel is God-ordained and we should be here. This is what God wants."

For a brief moment, the machines stopped churning up the sidewalk and I could hear birds singing in trees that grew out of circular holes in the walkways. Rittie began talking about a recent rift in an old friendship. She didn't say to what the argument pertained, but she was obviously still grieving; the hurt was still fresh. She confessed that she believed she had done everything she could to reconcile. But the gap between the two of them continued to widen. It was a tense time, she muttered out loud, and she wondered when to reconcile and when to shake the dust from her feet and move on.

"Reconciliation can't exist in a vacuum," she said, her voice gaining volume as she addressed me. I wasn't sure if she was now talking about the conflict of the land, or about her waning friendship. Perhaps both.

"We cannot reconcile unless we face the issues and the problems at hand," she continued. "We have to know each other and we must understand the other. We have to see each other *as* people. If things are ignored, the whole process will be put off balance, ignoring problems instead of digging them up and discussing them. Digging is painful because it makes you look at yourself in a society that perpetuates pain and injustice. To be sure, we are not the sole perpetuators. But, we cannot wait for the other to make steps. While we're singing *Hatikva* on Independence Day it's their catastrophe. This is why Musalaha is essential. It gives us a forum to discuss, to be heard and to hear, to be understood as well as to understand. Perhaps, from there, small steps can be taken. Perhaps."

Rachel Feinburg

I REPETITIVELY tapped my foot on the pavement, waiting. I was later than I had wanted to be, and it was my fault. I had traveled from Jerusalem earlier in the day, leaving Musalaha's office in Talpiyot and boarding a bus to Netanya. Once I arrived, I called Rachel Feinburg, who I was meeting, to let her know. "Oh no," she exclaimed, "I actually live in Kfar Saba, twenty minutes back in the other direction." I should have paid closer attention to her instructions. So I waited and found another bus that took me back from where I had come and dropped me off at the mall in nearby Kfar Yona, the easiest place for her to meet me.

A chilling wind swept down the street. I had hoped that the weather would get warmer as I got away from Jerusalem and closer to the coast. But this evening in Kfar Yona surprised me. I slipped on a long-sleeve shirt and huddled on the steps in front of the mall.

The darkness was deceiving; it was still quite early in the evening, and many people were filtering in and out of the mall doors. Young giggling couples and groups of teenagers wound around strollers and oblivious smokers chatting. I looked over to the road and a small, well-used car pulled over to the curb and the driver leaned across the passenger seat. I saw a hesitant wave in my direction and I hurried over to Rachel's vehicle.

"Oh, I'm glad it was you then," she said in a Yorkshire accent. "It would've been bad if I had just invited some random person into the car!"

We drove back through dark streets in quiet neighborhoods, and Rachel gave me a brief tour of her small community. The school system was respectable and playgrounds were built in long rows between lines of houses, away from the streets. She was very proud of the area, and she liked the gates. How safe and quiet it was, she said several times.

Rachel's parents were originally from the industrial north of England, where smokestacks grew like mechanized trees in once-quiet fields. Her father's job in the RAF (Royal Air Force) fortunately took the family to the green hills of Ireland, perfect for raising children, or so Rachel said. But the bombs and shootings forced them to Scotland when she was fifteen. Three weeks after they moved, the street where her father's work was located was bombed and burned to the ground along with five other houses.

Rachel came to Israel when she was twenty-one; she didn't like the cold, wet British weather and she hasn't looked back. She worked on a *kibbutz* near Akko for awhile, where she met her husband, and for the next two years they lived out of a mini-bus as they traveled through Europe. When they returned, her husband took a job at the Baptist Village as the Jewish director of their camps and conferences. Almost twenty years ago, he was using an electric saw on a big metal barrel that he didn't know still contained fumes. The sparks from the saw ignited the fumes and turned the barrel into a bomb. He was killed instantly.

Rachel stayed in the Baptist Village for six months after his death, and then moved with her three kids to Kfar Saba where she obtained a teaching qualification. Then she met a man who ran the swimming pool she frequented. One thing led to another, she said, and they got married, and she now has five children.

She pulled the little car into a narrow driveway and we squeezed into the front yard. Immediately, two dogs raced toward us and four paws began padding at my stomach, four glistening eyes blinked rapidly, and two tongues licked at my hands. Several more less-enthusiastic dogs, small Shetland sheepdogs, waited inside the door and gathered around my ankles as I sat at the kitchen table. They were a dog family, breeding and selling puppies. One of their pets was a champion from Spain, and his trophies from numerous competitions decorated the shelves in the modest, cozy kitchen. People pay for the privilege of their females mating with their champion dog. So, she joked, they run an animal prostitution ring as well.

A long-haired boy came stumbling out of a backroom, rubbing his eyes. He had finished his homework and he emerged for air, television, and food, apparently his third meal since supper. Her eldest daughter is studying media in Jerusalem, and is active in her congregation.

"They take everything literally at her congregation, at exactly face-value," Rachel said quite proudly. "If it says to pray for the sick, then they do. They believe that healing, miracles, and prophecy are for today, and not a thing of the past, and have many examples to prove this."

She turned her back to me and went to the small stove, scooping delicious steaming food onto a plate. I hadn't eaten anything the whole day and I wasn't opposed to food before conversation. Rachel sat at the other end of the table from me, slowly munching her own food and watching me curiously, asking questions about my home and my work with Musalaha. She wanted to know my story as much as I needed to know hers. Her long-haired son watched television in the living room behind us; flashes of colored light bounced off his mesmerized face and muffled sounds from a Disney Channel show became an undercurrent to our conversation. Rachel apologized that she didn't have any olives to offer. She teaches English in Arab communities, and some of the women give her jars of olives that are "to die for."

"Many of the people in these communities live in houses that Hollywood wouldn't be ashamed of," she said with a nod meant to convince. "Not all of them are poor victims, as the television loves to suggest. The Arabs I know have good jobs, are well dressed, and educated, and have small families. For them education is very important and many become doctors, chemists, and professionals in every field. Women are no longer expected to stay at home but are often highly qualified and most have jobs outside the home. However the press never shows this side of the story. Those I have spoken to are not interested in terrorism and believe that the problems can be solved through peaceful negotiations."

She carried our plates to the sink and ran water over. One of the dogs sat down under my legs and tilted its head toward me, not-so-subtlety begging for someone to scratch its ears. My family had a Shetland sheepdog named Molly, and she had been with our family since I was five. At the end of her life, she couldn't see, hear, and could barely move as arthritis ate at her joints. She died right before I came to work with Musalaha, at the age of twenty.

She told her son to turn the volume down. The words were now inaudible except for a low murmur and occasional ripples from the laugh tracks. Then she sat down and began talking.

"Twenty years ago, a Jewish believer was a very rare thing," she began. "Every year we would have a conference in the Baptist Village of all the believers in the land, and that was about four hundred people and you can scratch off half of them because they're like me: people from abroad. We knew everybody, but now each congregation is almost that big."

When she first came here, she knew next to nothing about any sort of conflict.

"I could always see it from both sides: there's one land and two people who both say it's theirs, and what's so clear is that they're both right. I could've easily married an Arab guy, because I didn't know the difference. I had never met a Jewish person until I came to Israel and knew nothing about the conflict. I was *completely* ignorant. The borders weren't there like they are now, and people could eat in Gazan restaurants, or do shopping in the markets in Tulkarem."

She loosened the scarf around her neck, and then her shoulders sank.

"Maybe I lived in ignorance, but the situation seems to have worsened. I'm more aware now," she exclaimed, not arrogantly but assuredly. "I read the newspaper and watch the news, but I certainly wasn't very aware of what was going on before I came. You live in a bubble. I'm married to a Jewish man, so we have no problems anywhere we go. Full citizenship for me, like I had in England. I didn't know all the little ways in which other people suffered. The press tells you what they want you to hear, and you live here and just don't know the other side."

She stared at the floor. Creased lines ran out from her eyes and her forehead furrowed.

"You just don't know. This is where Musalaha has really made a difference to me; it's my only opportunity to talk to women who live over the Green Line, and to hear firsthand about the difficulties they face. I feel that we are building relationships and our shared love of Yeshua is the most important thing—whether we are Arab, Christian, or Jewish is far less important than the real bond we have in Him. We see Him reflected in each other's eyes."

Four years ago, Rachel was invited to join Musalaha's Third-Side, a group for foreign women married to Israelis and Palestinians.

"Now don't forget," she urged, her hand extended in caution, "I was meeting Western women, not Arabs. So this wasn't, in a sense, the reconciliation that Musalaha is all about, I suppose. But you *could* feel vibrations; we had to be very careful not to offend each other. I could see that we had all come to identify with the side we married, and we weren't as neutral as we thought."

She smiled, pleased with her analysis. But she seemed aware that it included her.

"I don't think we realized how deeply we had become identified, thinking we were open-minded when we actually weren't. This group is very special because all of us, like Ruth, are committed to living here—'Where you go I will go, and where you stay I will stay. Your people will be my people and your God my God. Where you die I will die, and there I will be buried.' Our children are citizens of this country and they too have to struggle with identity issues. Primarily they need to be sure of their identity in the kingdom of God, and this is strengthened by involvement in the local congregations and by many summer camps, so that they know they belong to a big family of believers in this land. However the Third-Side group gives tremendous support to each of us as we seek to understand the differences in the society and culture we are living in. Each of us has a unique calling to be here, but that doesn't mean it's easy. This unique position is also the basis of what we bring to the work of Musalaha."

I asked her what she thought of the claim that Palestinians tend to accuse Musalaha of slightly pro-Israeli sentiments, while Israelis tend to assume that Musalaha appeases the Palestinian side.

"I can see why people could say that Musalaha has a more pro-Palestinian view," she answered, "but only because it *feels* like the balance is the wrong way because they are challenging the wider-known belief of a God-given right. Maybe they feel that the Jews needed to hear the other side more. It's not easy for all believers. Evan and Salim will tell you: you have to have many meetings before you can bring up politics. For a while, we wouldn't dare discuss political issues as Third-Siders."

One of the most meaningful conferences she attended last year was when two women, one Jewish and one Palestinian, shared their experiences in the Holocaust and the *Nakba*. Rachel insisted that the two historical incidents were not comparable; what was comparable though, was that these two suffering women chose to forgive.

"Both women's faces were just shining with love and forgiveness," Rachel whispered with profound respect. "It was a huge revelation for Arab women about the Holocaust. They hadn't been taught about it at school. On the other side, the *Nakba* was a revelation for the Israeli women because they believed everyone had left their homes and didn't know about people being forced out of their houses at gunpoint."

Rachel stood and went back to the connecting kitchen. She filled up a kettle at the sink and set it on the stove next to the cooling leftovers. She talked over her shoulder, telling me that she loved the Third-Side meetings, but that maybe some changes could be made.

"If you were to ask me what I would like, I would like for our meetings to include more talking with Arabs. I think what Musalaha's doing is very important. You have this whole generation who has been in the army, and it's important for them to meet the believers on the Arab side. My son was changed by his experiences in the army, and I'm thankful that he didn't have to shoot anyone. When boys are brought up as believers it can be very traumatic for them to be involved in combat."

The television was completely inaudible now. Or perhaps the sound was just beyond the edge of our attentions.

"The hopes for peace don't look that good."

Rachel's son had been stationed outside of Gaza during what Israelis call the Gaza War and Palestinians the Gaza Massacre, which erupted at the end of 2008. She had been afraid to go into the Arab villages where she taught, because people knew where her son was. The family of one of her students lives in Gaza. But when she came to teach the kids, the mother spoke to her with concern and asked "How's your son?" And Rachel asked "How's your family? Do they have any food?"

"It was really quite lovely," she said quietly.

The kettle behind her was steaming and she poured tea in two mugs and returned to the table.

She sighed, and looked around the room. The kitchen and living room, where the television still flickered, were not separated by any wall, and down a hallway to our right were bedrooms. A small patio lay out behind the window next to the table at which we sat. Two small dogs cuddled around my feet and kept them warm.

"I feel that being involved in something positive like Musalaha is important, and the best place to start reconciliation is in the Body. There could come a day when we'll all need to live in each other's homes if bombs are falling. If Arab believers and Jewish believers can't have peace, then who can?"

A chorus of syndicated laughter suddenly babbled from the television and Rachel chuckled along. She asked her son to turn the volume down a little more.

"Do you watch much T.V.?" she asked.

I told her that I didn't own a television, but my roommates and I did have quite a few things saved on computer hard-drives. She nodded and sipped the last of her tea.

"I never watched much at all," she explained, "but I've come to really enjoy watching Middle East TV. Ever heard of it? There's a Christian television station here, supported by that one American preacher . . . what's his name? He's on the 700 Club. Oh yes! Pat Robertson. Well, it's funded by him. I really enjoy watching Dr. Lester Sumrall as he is such a great Bible teacher."

Rachel's voice became more animated.

"He is always right on the money. The other day he talked about Israel, and it was just so insightful. He asked if we know why there's so much trouble here, why more people have been killed here than anywhere else in the world?"

I decided not to answer, so I shook my head. Rachel leaned forward determinedly.

"Dr. Sumrall said, 'Because God loves Israel; Satan hates it. This isn't a war between Arabs and Jews. This is a raging battle because Satan wants to destroy whatever God loves.'"

Pierre *and* Samar Tannous

THE EBENEZER House for the Elderly was very quiet at night, except for the electrical purring of a florescent light in the lobby corner. All other lights were off when I arrived. I was meeting with the pastor's wife of the Assemblies of God congregation and their oldest son the next day, and I crept to the top floor and found my room.

Pierre Tannous called me in the morning and said he was waiting outside. The morning was dim, but not overcast, and the air was cool with the possibility of rain. I tiptoed quietly down the stairs, although needlessly, because loud noises rang out from the kitchen at the bottom of the stairwell and aging tenants in bathrobes waited anxiously in the dining hall for breakfast. Pierre sat in a small car across the street. He was in his early thirties, a cleft in his chin, and he shook my hand warmly and welcomed me to Haifa. He started the car and we drove along the side street to the German Colony, a mostly Arab neighborhood at the foot of Mount Carmel. The main road to my right ran directly to the base, where the road met the Baha'i Gardens, flowing down the terraced mountain like a green waterfall. Pierre grew up in Haifa, and said the city had about 350,000 residents. He once attended the Anglican school, which he pointed out as we drove toward his home. Everyone went to chapel together, he said, even the Muslims.

"One time, the teacher asked who is Muslim in the class and some of the people raised their hands and that was the first time I knew the difference. To me, we were the same."

Pierre studied engineering at the Technion in Haifa. After graduation, Salim Munayer and Bishara Awad, the president of Bethlehem Bible College, approached him because they wanted more Palestinians to pursue advanced degrees in order to teach at the college. Pierre was unable to receive a scholarship from the U.S.; everything cost $25,000 per year, he said. A friend told Pierre to consider South Korea, which had excellent programs and was much cheaper. For the next three years, Pierre studied in an English-speaking seminary with students from all over Asia. He received a Masters of Divinity with a focus in ministry, and he now teaches Systematic Theology, Church History, and Old Testament. He used to teach once a week in Bethlehem, but now travels three days a week to villages in the north.

Pierre parked on a quiet street in the German Colony and we began walking toward his family's home. A row of apartments blocked out Mount Carmel. I was soon walking by myself; Pierre limped slowly behind me, favoring one leg. Several months before, he broke his ankle on a Musalaha trip to Norway.

"A group of us played some game where there's a pole with a hat on it," Pierre explained, and he laughed at himself. "And you have to jump up and kick the hat off the pole."

The hat came off and, when he landed, his ankle almost did too. He broke several small bones and tore two ligaments. He had been on crutches for months and was just learning how to walk again.

"So maybe we could walk a little slower," he grinned.

We walked up a set of stairs and entered a spacious apartment softly lit. Pierre's father Edward, the pastor of the Assembly of God, sat dressed in sweatpants in the living room. He stood to greet me, an older graying man with broad shoulders. Samar, Pierre's mother, prepared breakfast in the kitchen next to the front door. She wiped her hands on an apron and waved me to a seat.

Samar and Edward were both from Jish, a small northern village. Samar left for boarding school when she was fifteen, and after three years came to Haifa. Edward and Samar met in the village, but Edward's family moved to Haifa when he was twelve. She was nineteen when they met again and married. Samar studied Bookkeeping and Accounting in university and worked as a bookkeeper for seven years before becoming an accountant. However, she was let go this year because of the company's financial difficulties.

"First time I am home fulltime," she said, turning off the stove and washing her hands. "All the time I worked with Jews. My boss was Jewish. I know the other side because I was working with Jews and knew that their children were in the army. And I understood the fear they had. I tried to understand. But I would visit Bethlehem and Ramallah and I could see the injustice caused by the army, even as I tried to understand."

The table was set with tomatoes, eggs, zucchini, pita and hummus, and small Arabic pizzas spiced with thyme. Pierre said he used to have mouthwatering dreams about Arabic food when he was in Korea. After he returned, he gained seven kilos to make up for lost time. I told them about the book project and they asked about my family and home. Pierre translated for his father, who hunched forward and blinked constantly as he listened. Edward was more interested in what I thought about American churches. He talked quickly between mouthfuls of pizza and gulps of water.

After breakfast, Edward had work at the church building. Samar invited me into the living room where we could talk more comfortably. The dishes were washed, and her hands were still a bit wet, glistening when she moved them. She leaned back on the wide couch, drinking coffee from a small porcelain cup. She wiped a piece of fuzz from her black shirt, embroidered with a large red rose. Pierre sat on the adjacent couch, translating for his mother when needed. Her English was good, but she wasn't confident enough to carry the conversation by herself. Sometimes, when people are being translated, they understandably look at the person who is translating for them. But Samar looked at me. She nodded when she understood me and occasionally answered in English, but mostly she spoke softly in Arabic to Pierre and his voice conveyed her story.

"In the beginning," she said, and for a brief moment I wondered how far back she was actually going, "my grandfather was killed in 1948."

Jewish forces entered and occupied Jish, ordering all women and children to gather in the church. The men were outside when bombing and shooting erupted in the streets. A piece of shrapnel hit Samar's grandfather in the leg. He was taken to Lebanon for treatment, but they never saw him again. He died from an infected wound two months later. His wife was pregnant when he left, and Samar's mother was fifteen. But the family would not allow hate and prejudice to fester toward Jews. But the tense conflict was still strongly felt.

"At school," Samar said, "the Israelis would make us celebrate Independence Day, even though we are Palestinian and had our own schools. And when I was ten the Six Day War began. And we were told not to worry, because the Israeli Defense Forces were strong and would protect us because we were citizens too. When I left the village and began meeting Jews I realized that we were not treated the same. We had to get permits from the army to travel anywhere, like what's happening in the West Bank. We weren't seen as equal, even as equal citizens.

"When we grew up we stopped celebrating Independence Day and it was a conflict between the older and younger generations. The older was afraid and didn't want the younger generation to talk about politics, just to go, and study, and work. When I was seventeen, my school chose me to go to a conference for dialogue between Arabs and Jews, but my parents wouldn't let me go. They were afraid I would express myself in a way that would bring harm."

Samar's siblings attended university in Jerusalem and were very politically active, participating in nonviolent demonstrations. Samar put her finger to her lips.

"Shhh," she hushed, "my parents did not want this."

Samar first participated in a Musalaha family conference in 1998, where she met Evan Thomas and Salim Munayer. However, many people felt unable to express themselves in the midst of such large crowds. Around seven years ago, Musalaha formed more intimate smaller groups for women. Samar was one of the first to join.

"One of the most difficult experiences for me at Musalaha was sharing facts about 1948," Samar said. "Some of the Jewish sisters were shocked and said that these things weren't true. They said that the Jews never drove anyone out of their homes. That they just left. Even though at the same conference a Jewish lady came and spoke about the Holocaust, and Palestinians were not involved in this, and we felt very bad as she told her story. But when it came to 1948 both sides *were* involved. They said that the Palestinians just left."

She stopped for a moment and pinched the bridge of her nose. A ceramic clock on the wall ticked loudly in the silence. Pierre cleared his throat, glanced at me, and looked down at the carpet.

"But the fact is people *were* threatened," Samar said, nodding her head emphatically. "And this is why they fled. Most of the Jewish ladies involved in Musalaha's women's group were not born here, so they are just saying what they've been told. They think that when the army came to Arab villages they brought them food, and blankets, and treated people very kindly."

Samar smiled. She seldom moved as she talked, her legs crossed and her hands folded over them.

"And this might be true after they got independence. So they might have helped here and there. But the fact that people left because they were threatened is a historical fact. Because the Jewish sisters heard stories about an army who wanted to help people, they were shocked about stories of that same army who threatened and drove people out. Some of the Arab sisters said that the event of 1948 was still happening because the children of these Jewish women are in the military, in the checkpoints, and the tanks."

But the conference was also inspiring. The Holocaust survivor and Samia Shehadeh's mother, who told her experience in the

Nakba, spoke about forgiving their oppressors, a forgiveness made possible in its impossibility.

"This was one of the most difficult conferences for ladies. But also one of the most beautiful."

And even with the tensions and disagreements, Samar believes the friendships are the most encouraging part of Musalaha.

"In the last two wars, in Lebanon and Gaza, we used to call each other to ask about families and if everything was okay. During what happened in Gaza, there was a prayer meeting in Talitha Qumi for people from both sides. We are always emphasizing that we have a new identity in Christ, that we should understand one another, to learn what is happening on the other side.

"There is a big conflict in Musalaha of how we identify ourselves, and it can be a crisis. But we Palestinians want to explain to Israelis our identity so they understand us, and vice versa. As Arabs, there are many Arab countries, so we have Syrian Arabs, Lebanese Arabs."

One of her hands now unfolded itself from her lap and touched her heart. She spoke in English.

"And I am a Palestinian Arab living in Israel, and I told this to my Jewish friends and they were afraid of the word 'Palestinian.'"

Then she spoke again in Arabic: "I told them I belong to my culture and my tradition, that my roots are in the place that I live. There is no contradiction in being a Palestinian, and expressing yourself as such, and being a citizen in Israel."

"You know," she said, setting our coffee cups onto an engraved tray, "before going to Musalaha I didn't even know there was a conflict between Arab and Jewish believers. Sometimes, when my husband met between believers he could smell something in the atmosphere that just wasn't right. But I was raised in a way that if someone was a Christian, we believed that it didn't matter what ethnicity or nationality you were. You were a Christian. I thought Jewish believers would feel the same way, and not see a difference. I never thought about whose land is this, or if that issue had anything to do with spiritual matters.

"I thought that if a believer saw something unjust, or found out truth, they would respond to make it right. I was sharing breakfast with a Jewish lady in Musalaha, and she told me 'Don't you know God has given this land to the Jewish people according to the promise?'"

She closed her eyes and smiled.

"I thought that a Christian shouldn't be concerned with these matters."

I had asked few questions. Samar paused infrequently, like she already knew everything she wanted to share. I jumped in now: what do you think of the promise and why should a Christian not be concerned?

Samar paused now, thinking. The clock on the wall ticked and Pierre whispered something in Arabic. But Samar shook her head and began speaking again.

"In the Bible, there are promises connected to a condition. And these conditions are not being met. There are so many questions. And even Jews have questions about who is a Jew and how you decide this. I think the Jew is the one who is following God. That's why the promise of the land is a bit difficult to interpret. And I understand that they want to hold on to the promise, but only if the conditions are met."

She suddenly laughed and her shoulders bounced up and down.

"Maybe we'll be in heaven by then! But this land, everything above it, and below it, belongs to God. Whatever we speak about, we want to go back and see what Jesus wants us to do, to be one in Christ. One of the things I had problems with in the beginning, but that I accept now, is that they don't celebrate Christian feasts, but they do celebrate feasts in the Old Testament. But I accept this now. And one of the most beautiful experiences was when we all shared communion together. It was a powerful and profound experience. You feel in that moment that you are one."

Samar left soon after we finished talking. She had many errands to run. Pierre and I remained in the living room. The house was quiet. Every now and then, we heard raindrops gently flicking against the window and cars splashing through puddles in the street. Pierre grabbed two cups and a bottle of juice from the kitchen, then propped his leg up as he sat down on the couch.

"In 1987," Pierre said, "when the first *intifada* began, I didn't really know anything about the conflict. Growing up here in Haifa helped that. In Haifa, we don't have soldiers or border guards, so we don't have this experience of someone oppressing you all the time.

"And then the numbers of people dying in the *intifada* began rising, and we saw images on the screen of soldiers beating young Palestinians, smashing their hands with stones. I was very emotional and began becoming more nationalistic in my ideas. My ideas about Jews at that time were very negative."

He took a sip of juice and slightly rotated his leg. It was healing, he said, but he moved his foot delicately and occasionally winced.

"Several years later, I'm not really sure when, I was reading a book by Khalil Gibran, just very short sayings and parables. And one of them said 'If you have thorns in your heart, how can you expect to have flowers in your hands?' If I hated Jews, how could I love anyone?"

Pierre shrugged and smiled, and said, "So I decided that I should love everyone."

His first experience with Musalaha was the same family conference in Tantur that his mother mentioned. And like Samar, he was unaware of the tensions between Christians on both sides.

"I remember wondering why we even needed this. We are all Christians. But I bought a book Salim edited about opinions of people from both sides and I was shocked. Growing up in Haifa, on the political map, people were usually on the left and I shared views with them. So I thought surely people who followed Jesus would be too. I was so shocked that they thought the land belonged to them. I don't remember many other specific things, but the tone and the perspective itself was surprising. To me it was clear: the Jews came back, and eventually took over the land, and occupied it. And that's fine, well, it's a fact. But don't tell me the Bible says this is the will of God and according to God's plan."

Pierre's voice remained calm, but he squirmed and his eyes narrowed.

"This was a little too much for me."

After reading the book, instead of reacting bitterly, Pierre channeled his discomfort. He wanted to hear and understand more, to discuss what was happening in this small strip of land.

"We may have different views, but we are one family and we shouldn't forget that. I don't think we should give our differences the dominant role in our Christian community. And most of the time, at these conferences, I felt that people aren't feeling angry about the differences, but are feeling sad by what they are learning."

Pierre taught a session during a young adult conference in Turkey. He based his lesson on a text central to Musalaha, in Ephesians: the Christ has destroyed the dividing wall of hostility. But, Pierre asked, are we rebuilding it with the way we live our lives?

"And the Palestinians talked about how this wall was being built, *literally*," said Pierre, "but the Israelis had a difficult time deciding whether or not there was a wall. The Palestinian side feels this harder because they experience the conflict every day. I'm not saying that Jews don't feel the conflict, because everyone has a relative who is a soldier somewhere. But maybe they don't feel it every day."

And yet sometimes cracks are created and views through the holes are visible. While at a Musalaha meeting, Pierre overheard a conversation between two Jewish guys and a Palestinian. One of the Jews said that, while he was in the military, he shot two Palestinians who were entering a settlement. He killed them. And then he said that he looked into the face of one of them and realized that he was no older than sixteen. This was the face of someone he could have known. The Palestinian then shared his side of the story, and why he thinks some Palestinians do things like that.

"They were seeing," Pierre said. "They were seeing that the other side is not just a soldier, or a terrorist, but a human being."

We took a break from the conversation during the afternoon. Pierre needed to prepare lesson plans for his classes on Monday, and I could always type notes and send emails. We sat working in a balcony turned into a study with potted plants and bookshelves. My interview scheduled for the evening was cancelled, so when Pierre finished tweaking his curriculum, he took me on a driving tour of Haifa. We drove to the top of Mount Carmel and looked down on the cascading Baha'i Gardens. Lights in the city flickered on around the rim of the mountain, fireflies swarming in the bowl of the valley. As the sun went down, we watched light and wind hover over the surface of the waters, and tremors of waves like wrinkles on a glass sea. Colors spread out from the horizon and faded high above our heads into growing darkness. Pierre stood next to me, his hands in his pockets, shifting from foot to foot. I told him that Musalaha has been labeled pro-Palestinian among many Messianic Jewish groups, and for that reason Musalaha often feels hindered in how far and how soon they can push certain issues. Pierre shifted again and shook his head.

"Hmmm," he murmured, and remained silent for a few moments. Then he continued. "For people to say that you are pro one way, they think you must be anti another. This doesn't have to be the case. A zero-sum mentality isn't going to change anything.

"Meeting believers from all backgrounds has changed me at least. And I saw that people are living the Christian life in various ways, other than how I am living. And it's okay. I've heard Jewish kids sharing good things about Arabs in their schools, and the little daughter of a friend of mine, who I met at Musalaha, said she should learn Arabic. When I get married and have children, will I teach them the same openness?"

Sudden winds knocked us back a few steps. The colors had mostly disappeared as the darkness overhead melted down to the horizon.

"Musalaha is not doing a work of just bringing people together and being happy," Pierre said. He turned toward me, but kept looking at the waves whose sound we couldn't hear. "Musalaha doesn't take a position of judging which side is more right. It is just trying to get both sides to be open to the other side. When a person says they were treated inhumanely at the checkpoint, you can't say 'no you weren't.' And when you say you were terrified from a suicide bombing attack you can't say 'no you weren't.' Israel is here and it's a historical fact. There were and are injustices, people losing water, and land, and we should speak about these things. But I don't want to connect this Israel to the Bible. It's here to stay, but not because of the Bible. We need to let people from outside share in these experiences and let them decide where there is right and wrong."

Yousef Khalil

M<small>Y LEGS</small> were burning as I hiked up the steep incline from Beit Sahour to Bethlehem. My house sits on a secluded hill, and is one of the only buildings on its lonely summit. I had recently found a shortcut between the two towns, climbing steadily and more steeply up until it comes through the back of Manger Square. Flickering streetlamps cast a cold light on the cracking stone. Cars raced from one side to the other on the narrow strip of road as kids ran back and forth kicking a deflated football, stopping to unconvincingly beg for shekels from assumed tourists. I walked down through the dark Old City, past closed shops and silhouetted pedestrians dodging decrepit trucks in the cramped streets. Taxis swarmed like flies around Bab-Izqak, honking in failed attempts to entice me for a ride. I moved to the right along Hebron Road and stopped opposite the Latin Patriarchate School, beneath an apartment building. Yousef Khalil stuck his face out of a balcony window on the third floor and directed me to the door.

Yousef stood on the landing in the dark; the light bulb was burned out. We had met several times before and he greeted me warmly with a firm handshake. He was as tall as me, over six feet, with wide shoulders. He had a broad, toothy grin that glistened amidst a dark scraggly beard, spreading down his neck to tufts of chest hair beneath his sleeveless white undershirt. He wanted to shave, he said.

"The beard itches like crazy!" he said, his thick Arabic accent emphasizing the 'r's.

He led me inside his sparse apartment and over ruffled mattresses on the floor to a small table by the balcony window. I could hear incessant car horns and screeching wheels from Hebron Road, orange under streetlamps and pinpoints of light from the refugee camp.

"It is difficult to sleep here," Yousef said, pointing to one of the mattresses on the floor. "Always this noise, all night long!"

Yousef looked down at his laptop to answer the quick pop of someone chatting on Facebook. A pungent smell of mint-and-apple tobacco wafted from the unlit *argileh*, hookah, that sat on the floor next to my feet. Corn-on-the-cob lay half-eaten on a plastic plate next to an open box of pastries from The Golden Bakery. "*Yalla*, go," Yousef said, watching me eye the pastries. One of his roommates was tucked in one of the mattresses, watching *Doctor Dolittle* on an old television in the corner. Except for the table, the mattresses, and a few chairs, the apartment had no furniture and looked bigger because of the unfilled space. It looked like the dorm rooms of some of my friends in university, with more litter and less room. And it felt familiar and homey.

Yousef and his six siblings were raised in a Catholic family in Zebabdeh, a village near Jenin, where his parents still live.

"My family is from there for a loooong time," he said, drawing his arms apart. "Before 1948."

He studied theology at Bethlehem Bible College, which was just down the street from us.

"I am now studying for a Masters in institutional building," he said, fiddling with a small cross around his neck. "I think institutional building . . . I don't know, it's the same as Raed."

I think Raed called it Organization Management and Development.

"Yeah, yeah, whatever, same thing," Yousef said smiling.

He looked out the window frequently as he talked, his eyes following the cars and the people yelling loudly late at night.

During his first semester at BBC, Yousef began looking for a job because his parents were unable to help with money. His new friend Raed showed him the work at Jemima, and Yousef immediately felt called to work with these children. After awhile, Yousef learned of needed help at the House of Hope, near the Bible College, and he left to work with them for two years. But some issues arose with the director and Yousef is now working fulltime with Jemima again. He had recently organized a festival through Musalaha for different organizations for the developmentally disabled.

"These places have to give me some change," he said, leaning intensely forward with both hands holding the computer screen. "I have to feel about them, about the children, and think about them. In society, we don't see them, *ya'ani*, we don't involve them in what we do. And now I live and work with them. This has to change me."

Yousef has become close with the children he serves, including one boy with epilepsy and severe mental retardation. He was found in a Bedouin village in the north, chained to a pole in front of his family's tent. The boy's parents are both mentally handicapped and ostracized from their own families. They had no idea how to care for their son, no way to understand what was happening to him. Yousef wanted to do a Masters in Speech Therapy because of his relationship with this boy, but no such program exists in Palestine.

Yousef stood and leaned against the window. He rubbed his bare arms as he peered down to the shadowed alleys. His roommate turned down the volume on the TV; Eddie Murphy gasped as a hamster started singing and dancing. I asked Yousef about his childhood in Jenin.

"I saw tanks in front of my eyes," he said, still staring out the window. "Planes, checkpoints, soldiers with guns and I faced it. But, I would not hate them or fight them. My parents raised me this way, and then I began to have my own faith and I began to believe in love and forgiveness. It comes together, you know, faith and parents. But there are things in my heart I cannot forget."

He put his hand on his chest.

"When I was ten or twelve years old, there were Israeli attacks near Jenin. My friend and I were playing football in the street and the soldiers attacked us and tied our hands. I didn't understand this. I'm a young kid and you do this to me? When the army came to Jenin, during the massacre, all the tanks and cars came through my village to shoot and destroy."

He stopped for a moment and lowered his head. He had spoken quickly, and more loudly as he continued. He came back to the table and typed something on his computer. The glow from the screen lit his face in dull blue. He pushed the laptop away from him.

"And I thought: in a few minutes, children, and parents, and people will die, and I can't stop this. I could do nothing."

When the second *intifada* erupted, he said, it would take him eight or nine hours to go from Bethlehem to Zebabdeh, around eighty kilometers apart and is normally a three-and-a-half hour drive. He and his friends would hide under olive trees at two in the morning, holding their heads between their knees as they waited for a taxi.

"We couldn't light a cigarette because if they see it" - he whistled and shot his hand toward me, like a bullet. "I remember doubting if I am in life or not. I'm in this world, but I'm not living my humanity."

He dug his hand into his chest, like he was burrowing for that humanity.

Then, soon after this, Shireen Hilal, one of the leaders of Musalaha's women's groups, came to him and told him about a possible position doing youth work. He was worried at first, because of what people in Zebabdeh might think about Musalaha. Maybe they would think he was conspiring with the enemy, leaking information. He asked advice from his family and several close friends before saying "*Hallas*, okay." In August 2007, he began a year-long stint with Musalaha.

"I was a sort of coordinator under Shireen," he explained, "to arrange things like meetings and projects. It gives me a lot of help, especially now for Jemima. I never thought of being coordinator for a group. It was funny to coordinate people older than me, telling them 'Go here' and 'Do this!'"

He hunched forward and rubbed his hands together, chuckling mischievously.

Yousef took training courses in biblical geography and the Middle East conflict. Yousef helped teach the youth to confidently stand in front of a group and share their stories, which in turn aided him: Musalaha sent him to Denmark, speaking in churches about his experiences with the organization and encounter with his "other"—Israelis. He had already believed, but he now saw, that whatever humanity was buried in him was also buried in the Israelis.

"I go to the checkpoint and it's long, and I'm tired, and angry, and I should be angry, but I say '*Hallas*, I have Jewish friends now. I cannot hate the people.'" He rested his chin on his hands and added with a smile: "I'm kind of a peaceful man."

Yousef moved near the *argileh*, lighting several coals and placing them on the tinfoil. He blew softly and nudged the coals over pinpricked holes in the foil. I told him about Raed's concern for justice and with what he perceived to be Musalaha's silent voice.

"One side is occupying and oppressing the other and this we cannot forget," Raed had told me. "I believe we can live together, but we are not equal: we are under occupation. We are not both suffering in the same way."

Yousef leaned back, the hose from the *argileh* tucked between his folded arms. He scratched his forehead with the mouthpiece and then sat up sharply.

"Musalaha is, in a way, not political." He shook his head. "*Ya'ani*, everything is political. I mean, we only hear about justice in a political way, you know, this is my land, you are doing this bad thing to me, and you should pay for it. And yes, we should talk about this, about the Occupation."

He smiled and shook a prophetic finger in the air.

"But there is other justice too and we can't forget it. If I'm going to follow justice in this political way, then I will expect society's ways to work. But in faith, I have to follow this other justice . . ."

His shoulders sank and he sighed, frustrated at his inability to articulate. But suddenly he jumped back in.

"I'm not giving you two definitions, because for me it's one justice, but we and society do this justice in very different ways. To me, justice is 'Let's live together in this land, let's love one another, and when I need help you help me, when you need help I help you.' Justice is like brothers. I don't mean that we forget all the bad things. I mean, this land is mine . . ."

He put his hand once again on his heart, but then extended it to me.

" . . . but at the same time it's yours. This is ours, because we all use it and need it now. This is true justice."

Does he have hopes for this distributive justice to become a reality?

Yousef answered immediately.

"Sure. I have hope. If not, then I'll do nothing and start smoking marijuana."

He burst into peals of laughter, slapping my hand with a loud clap. He wiped his eyes and blew on the coals again. He still hadn't started smoking.

"I wish I had money to give to people whose families have died in *intifada*," he said quietly, his voice lowering as he became more serious. "I wish, sometimes, I could be God and stop all these rules, and wars, and start . . . and start a new life, a new testament."

He was almost speaking to himself now and he looked out the window, his arms still crossed. He seemed drawn to the window, to the idea of open space offering freedom from confinement.

"Just live it," he said, nodding. "Let's build on the small things. Muslims know Christ in a different way, so let's build on this. It's not just the political leaders: this situation is me, it's you, it's him, it's my mother and father, and it's them."

Yousef stood and walked to the window, shaking his fist, and he shouted "Justice! Welcome!"

A chorus of car horns responded. And then the night was still. Yousef turned to me with a broad, toothy grin and said, "You know Jericho? Maybe we can walk around this Wall seven times . . ."

Epilogue

W HEN I first began brainstorming for this epilogue, I thought that I would reflect very specifically. I planned on challenging some of the disconcerting perspectives shared. Like any other reader, I heard views that disturbed me and I heard misrepresentations of history and of current events. I thought, perhaps, I would amend some of those misrepresentations. But in such limited space, I could not adequately dive into such complexities without doing them severe injustice. And even if I could, should I? We must challenge and we must respond, but I'm not sure that mixing my voice too explicitly into this collection of narratives is appropriate. And even less appropriate toward the end. At least for this specific project, Pierre Tannous is correct: "We need to let people from outside share in these experiences and let them decide where there is right and wrong."

Then I thought that perhaps I would respond more generally; instead of pinpointing quotes, I would highlight themes that arose, drawing on differences between Israeli society and Palestinian society. But again, limited space, and lack of training, prohibits careful exploration into cultural issues without doing them severe injustice. Furthermore, general responses prove very difficult without a locus point from which to move or respond. Without specificity I have none.

Instead, I will briefly reflect on myself and on my impressions of the stories and the people involved.

I heard difficult stories and difficult opinions. They challenged me, frustrated me, and nourished me. Through the entire process, as I conducted the interviews, typed the notes, and wrote the stories, I was continually confronted with opinions different than my own, offering nuances to my views. I was forced to consider the experiences of those with whom I spoke. My preconceived notions were called into question. I had to take those notions apart and consider the pieces. I had to allow myself to be eroded by other perceptions of realities. It was difficult. It was challenging, frustrating, and it was nourishing. And it was necessary, because I saw faces, learned names, and heard stories. Deconstruction, for them and for me, is given room to happen in those moments.

But even though I met and interviewed these people, had coffee and tea and meals with them, and stayed in some of their homes, I didn't really get to know most of them. I've only seen many of them one time. And most of them didn't really get to know me. Who we say we are is often an idealized representation of ourselves, because we don't want just anyone to know what we hide. But there is still room for humble deconstruction of our edited narratives. When we openly and willingly place our narratives next to the narratives of others, which these people did, the cracks become visible. Loving our enemies does not mean that we will always like what we find out. It does not mean that just because we hear the other story that we must accept everything involved and disagreement will magically be erased. Loving our enemies, which includes recognizing the enemy in us that we project, is about radical transformation. Who we are is not what we believe or say about ourselves. Who we are is what we do, what we give up, what we live in the faces of our enemies. Participating in this constant action is an invitation to continually let go and be filled with something different.

Difference is how we learn. From before I can remember, my dad taught me to always speak with the possibility that I could be wrong (a discipline which I have never, and will never, master). My dad also taught me that, instead of only interpreting the world through the lens of the Bible, I should also interpret the Bible through the lens of the world. When I read those ancient, sacred texts, I must keep in mind the experiences of "the least of these," because they will be affected by my interpretations. I read with tension and the knowledge of difference and diversity. These stories are, in that extremely small way, like the Hebrew Scriptures, which make room for truth to happen in the cacophony of diverse experiences. Moses' theology does not fit comfortably with Job's. But in the struggle, in wrestling with God and with others, we discover meaning and the chaff begins to fall away.

I felt that struggle when I listened to these people speak, and I tried to open myself to it. I often felt drained afterward. And while I did not and cannot agree with some viewpoints, or even some worldviews, I have to recognize where many of these people have come from and where they are now, and where they hope to keep going. In my opinion, some have further to go than others. Some have more to let go of than others. But they have come further than they were before, and they have let go of more than they had before. In the midst of disagreement and concern, I can and must recognize that. I would want them to think the same thing of me. We are all on this journey.

I respect the people I interviewed. I looked again, and kept looking again as I wrote and rewrote. I respect them because most of them did not offer grandiose tales or exaltations about themselves. Most of them spoke with humility, even humiliation over things they have previously thought and done. Many spoke with the assumption that they could be wrong and that they might even think differently in the future. Some were not sure that their stories were "exciting" or "compelling" enough to tell. They seemed to recognize that who they are is not defined by what they say in this interview, but by what they go on, and out, to do.

Every one of the people in these stories is, in varying degrees, involved with Musalaha. And they are involved because they share a commitment to a redemptive narrative about a kingdom, a way, a banquet table where there is neither male nor female, rich nor poor, Jew nor Arab, Israeli nor Palestinian. This is not promoting an imperialistic dominance that annexes diversity into a colorless uniformity. Israelis do not have to become Palestinian, and Palestinians do not have to become Israeli. In the midst of heated debates about identities we must remember that in order for us to find our identity we must first lose it. And not because after losing our identity we will find it, but because the act of losing is finding.

I hope these stories will help us to engage in that act, because it is necessary for reconciliation to occur. Reconciliation, which in its Latin origins means "to make good again," is like fertile ground, because in it forgiveness is made possible. In order to overcome old prejudices we must be converted to a new one: the prejudice of love for the other whose face we are now coming to see, whose name we are now coming to understand, and whose story we are now coming to hear. May we have those ears to hear and those eyes to see. Peace, *shalom*, and *salaam*.

Reflections

Four Reactions from Israelis and Palestinians

LISA LODEN

As I read the stories recounted in *Reflections, You Have Heard It Said: Events of Reconciliation*, I was moved many times by the soul wrenching struggle of the narrators. Each story was deeply personal as the contributors shared their struggles of what it means to be Palestinian Christians and Messianic Jews, reconciling to one another, in the multi-faceted, conflicted reality that is Israel and Palestine. Jonathan MacRay has done an excellent job of transcribing these personal stories, bringing each one to life through his vivid descriptions of the people, their settings, and their stories.

If there is a common thread weaving through the diverse narratives it is the honest grappling with issues of faith and reconciliation that went on in the hearts and was reflected in the telling of their stories. Reconciliation—*musalaha, ritzui*—the process, is not only about interpersonal relationships. The process and the struggle are often to find ways of integrating faith, scripture, history, and personal experience. Different theologies and worldviews are the underlying background of the stories, coloring each perspective with subtle washes of meaning.

Every story contained a challenging personal encounter with "the other side" and most credited Musalaha with providing a safe environment for this to happen. The desert, as neutral ground, stripped as it is of comfort and outside the routine of daily life, was often the context for beginning breakthroughs. Regardless of the initial reason for accepting the invitation to participate in the desert experience, the expansive stillness of the desert provided the environment for openness and intimacy to begin to develop naturally. It was in this stripped down place with no escape hatch that the participant began to see the "other" as someone very like himself. The stillness of the desert enabled listening and the stories repeatedly highlighted this dynamic. Listening was often the first step of the journey. Listening and truly hearing the painful stories of the other required openness and a hearing of the heart. Another function served by the desert was to facilitate the process of "emptying" of preconceived ideas, stereotypes and fears about the "other." Musalaha's use of the desert as the setting for intentional encounters is clearly a successful factor in the reconciliation journey.

All the individuals interviewed faced, and dealt with, significant challenges to their identities and or ideologies. Identity is never an issue until it is challenged. Meeting with "the other," the one who is unlike you and even "an enemy," challenges personal identity, theology, and ideology. All the stories related a process of reexamination of identity and/or national history. It was interesting to note how frequently hearing another perspective challenged, and changed the individual's view of himself, and the other. With challenges to identity, the participants had to see themselves in a wider perspective in relation to other equally valid identities that sometimes were at odds with their own. Musalaha helped in initiating this process, providing the framework for the individuals to later work through the issues themselves. The role of Musalaha here was to question without providing answers. This approach challenges the individuals themselves to take responsibility to further the reconciliation process. Musalaha's role needs to continue being catalytic rather than prescriptive.

The issue of the theology of the land repeatedly surfaced in the stories. The sides are unmistakably divided in their understandings and perspectives. For many of the Jews interviewed, the land is promised by God to the Jewish people and belongs to Israel. This is non-negotiable. Relating to the Palestinians who hold another view of scripture is challenging and often painful for the Jewish Israelis and those who identify with them through marriage. The Palestinians do not see the issue in the same way but there is some variety as to how the land issue is perceived. In their view, issues of justice are much more prominent. Musalaha could provide a framework for theological aspects of this question to become part of the discussion. Building personal connections and then, on that relational basis, Musalaha could facilitate deeper discussion of theological issues. Several of those interviewed indicated that the theological questions are under discussed in Musalaha. Perhaps the relational ground is not yet sufficiently strong as Musalaha has yet to rise to the challenge of deep theological discussion. Since Musalaha works primarily within a faith based framework, these issues need to be brought forward at some point if the process of reconciliation is to advance.

On the personal level, that was part of all of the stories, the contributors to this book centered on their individual faith perspective. For each one, this focus brought them to a place of openness and acceptance of their brothers and sisters who come from different ethnic backgrounds and whose national aspirations are incompatible with their own. The love of God, their common shared humanity, identification with the pain of the other, forgiveness, and commitment to pursuing the relationships birthed in Musalaha are both the starting point and ongoing path for the reconciliation journey. Musalaha needs to remain conscious of this dynamic over the long term.

Another important theme emerged in many of the stories. This was the theme of courage, and the place, and power of decision. Again and again phrases like *"I decided not to live in fear"* or "*I decided to love everyone*" appeared in the stories. Many times, those interviewed spoke of their fears or the potential risks involved in coming together with the other side. People exhibited amazing willingness to be vulnerable. Each person evidenced great courage in opening to the pain of their brothers and sisters from the other side. Sometimes this was accompanied by a sense of confusion and shame on account of what their ethnic group had done. There appears to be a need to deal with issues of shame and guilt in Musalaha encounters. Teaching focus on the importance and power of personal decision in the reconciliation process could also be helpful.

Musalaha's choice of small groups rather than a conference format underscored the importance of close personal interaction. This format served to enable deeper levels of intimacy. Sharing in small groups helped the participants to be open and honest with one another. The fact that these groups continue over years is also a positive factor. Musalaha would do well to continue using and expanding this format. A further suggestion might be to explore the possibility of special focus or special activity groups in addition to the current format.

I discerned a disheartening trend emerging from the stories. While some levels of hopefulness were expressed, there was also an undercurrent of dissatisfaction with the current state of things. For some this came through in their final statements that reinforced their previously held theological understandings. For others, it came through in tentative statements about the possibility of peace. Musalaha faces a challenge to encourage and build up a sense of hope in the individual participants. This will not be easy since the socio-political context remains unpredictable and unstable.

Musalaha has contributed a great deal to the vital work of reconciliation between Messianic Jews and Palestinian Christians. Much, however, remains to be done. Reconciliation is a journey. The stories in *Reflections, You Have Heard It Said: Events of Reconciliation* poignantly express the beauty, pain, and challenge of the journey. Musalaha can continue to expand its initiative, involve others, and learn from the successes, challenges, and questions that are raised by these and other stories. My hope is that, because of this book, there will be many others who will choose to begin the journey and share their stories.

MUNTHER ISAAC

In reading these stories, it becomes clear that both sides bring with them preconceived perceptions about the other. These conceptions are shaped through the person's personal experience and their own society. For most Israelis, their first encounter with Palestinians was during their military service. For the Palestinians, their first encounter with Israelis was with an Israeli soldier. We cannot understand the dynamics of these *musalaha* (reconciliation) encounters if we do not take this point into consideration. It is never easy for a person to rid himself of these preconceived stereotyping. Everyone brings this to the first encounter. This must change in order to achieve *musalaha*.

For the Palestinian therefore, the other is the enemy, the occupier and oppressor, the one who built the wall. He is the soldier who stops him at the checkpoint. The other is the one they used to hate. For the Israelis, the other is the one who shoots at their neighbourhoods, the one they fight while serving in the military, and the reason why they live in fear.

Palestinians have stories. Lots of stories! They travel daily through checkpoints, they (or their family members) have been arrested, they are looked down at, humiliated, discriminated against, or have gone through a traumatic experience. All this has shaped their view of the other. The checkpoint, the wall, and stories like these ones told in this book create an inner image of the other and of self. "We are not equal," the Palestinian thinks. "I hated a thing called Israeli soldiers."

For the Palestinian, the issue is justice. They are willing to forgive and reconcile, but only if there are signs of repentance or at least compassion from the other side. They feel victimized. They want an apology. Nothing short of that will satisfy them. This is what they seek first in these encounters. What Musalaha achieves for them is that it introduces them to a new "other"—an Israeli who feels with them, who is sorry for what the soldiers are doing, and who are themselves ashamed of having been soldiers at a point in their lives. Because of this new friend, the Palestinian is now even willing to put aside the theological differences, and is ready for *musalaha*. He is ready now to see the soldier as a "young kid" who is not necessary evil by nature. He is willing to see now that there might be good soldiers, and that Israelis suffer as well.

I suspect the Palestinian will not be willing to move on with *musalaha* or forgive if the other he encounters does not show signs of compassion or repentance. The Palestinians will not accept any theology that does not show elements of justice—this is because of their experiences (stories). Don't tell them that "the Bible says this is the will of God and according to God's plan." In order for *musalaha* to take place for the Palestinian, it is not enough if the other is a Christian. The other must feel with their pain, understand their narrative, and realize their plea for justice.

Whereas Palestinians have stories, the Israelis rely more on their theology. The Israeli's theology is what created their narrative. Their move in the first place (*aliyah*) to Israel was because of their theological belief about the land, people, and covenant. They feed on this.

However, there is a clear tension in the minds and hearts of the Israelis who shared their stories. On one hand, their theology tells them that they belong to the land, that this is their God-given land, and that they are part of the "ingathering of the Jewish people." On the other hand, there are the Palestinian Christians, their brothers, and sisters in Christ, who remind them of the tragic consequences of their theology. When Israelis encounter Palestinian Christians their Christian ethics and conscious are challenged. They, however, do not allow the encounter to challenge their theology, because to do so would be to challenge "what they needed to believe in order to live here." And so there is tension.

Faced with this challenge and tension, Israelis have to keep reminding themselves of their theology (which is really their narrative). Almost all of them are first or second generation immigrants to Israel (who made *aliyah*). They do not know "how things work politically," and they are really sorry for the consequences. But there are no regrets; no denying the fact God is on their side. But God is on the Palestinian Christian's side as well. This is the dilemma.

And, so, many choose to continue denying Palestinian suffering. They continue to treat the Palestinian's story with suspicion, and say for example that "Palestinians just left on their own" in 1948. It is understandable that Musalaha is therefore viewed by some as pro-Palestinian. I believe this is simply a way of dodging the challenges raised by the Palestinian Christians. Whereas those who participated and continue to do so from the Israeli side call themselves "leftists," the ones on the "right" do not want to subject themselves to the challenge of having to reconcile their theology with what is happening in the Palestinian territories. Some said that in their first encounter they felt uncomfortable and that the Palestinians were trying to make them feel guilty. But the real radicals in my mind are those who choose to continue doing *musalaha* and to try somehow to make sense of their identity, theology, and practice. They are the true radical followers of Christ.

Meeting in the desert, on an "equal" ground is an exceptional idea. People from both sides expressed this in direct and indirect ways. The first encounter must serve to bring both sides together on neutral ground. Palestinians communicate a sense of "inferiority" or feeling "unequal" or "oppressed," whereas Israelis bring their fears and military experience with them. There is a lot of ice-breaking and wall-breaking to do before any talk of *musalaha* can be done. The desert serves to strip us of the physical things that divide us. There are no soldiers in uniforms, no masked people, no nice clothes, no poor or rich. The desert brings us down to the ground level, the foundation of what makes us human.

Perhaps Palestinians and Israelis come to these desert encounters hoping to change the "other." The amazing thing about these stories is that almost everyone shared how a major change took place, not in the other, but in himself. Whether it is a "softening in the heart," or a "transformation of our passions," or something that "cleansed the soul," or the realization that "I cannot hate anymore" God is in the business of changing hearts, preconceived perceptions, and stereotypes. This is where *musalaha* begins. Reconciliation begins when God starts changing *us* first to see the other through new eyes. The most radical of changes is that we move *from hate to love* and acceptance.

In the midst of all these difficulties, *musalaha* continues to take place. Despite the fears, inner tensions, struggle to accept and forgive, and despite the despair and lack of hope in peace, *musalaha* press on. Despite the different theologies and the disagreements, *musalaha* moves forward. Why? How come? Because these Christians have come to realize that "through the commonality of a shared faith," *musalaha* is possible. Because these Christians take seriously the command in 1 John 4:20 that says whoever says he loves God but hates his brother is a liar. They take Eph 2:14–16 seriously. They began to see not just that the other is a human made in the image of God, but they also see now that the other has value.

They also see the need to forgive and reconcile. The world needs it. For "if Arab believers and Jewish believers can't have peace, then who can?" Or as our Lord Jesus himself prayed in John 17:21, "that all of them may be one, Father, just as you are in me and I am in you. May they also be in us "so that the world may believe that you have sent me."

PHILIP BEN-SHMUEL

First of all, I want to thank my friend Jonathan McRay for pouring himself into this project. I know the process of writing and editing these stories was at least as challenging and frustrating as the encounters themselves—I hope the process was also nurturing. These beautifully and skillfully written stories are captivating snapshots of Christian and Messianic life in Israel and Palestine. I also appreciate Jonathan's unwavering emphasis on justice. It is a demanding ideal which we all inevitably interpret somewhat differently. Yet, justice summons us all to respect the interpretation of our sisters, and brothers, and enemies—to look again, and then again. These snapshots draw us into that cycle of respect, if only we open our eyes to looking again.

These stories revealed a few really encouraging strengths in Musalaha's work and progress. Several of those interviewed mentioned that many of their early encounters with the "other side" were in a military environment—either as a soldier or as a person feeling oppressed by soldiers. Militaries, due to their very nature and purpose, engage in some dehumanization, both of the soldiers and of the "enemy." Musalaha's desert encounters have had such success because the desert is a place where the balance of power is neutralized and people are able to "see each other *as* people," as one of the interviewees put it. One of the Israeli young adults who participated in such a desert encounter reflected that "the opposite of dehumanization happens real fast." This is perhaps best epitomized by the young Palestinian who, on account of the oppression he encountered, "hated the thing called Israeli soldiers," but in the desert he was able to find blessing, comfort, and cleansing by the voice and touch of an Israeli soldier who was also his brother. As we read, this rehumanization leads sometimes to very genuine and life-changing friendships. These relationships prove more powerful than any political or theological lecture or agenda—they are what enable empathy, give shape to our complex and composite identities, and lead us towards acts of love.

But this process of reconciliation is still very obviously a work in progress. There are several "separation barriers" dividing us which sometimes feel just as tangible as the one made of wire and concrete snaking through the West Bank. I will briefly point to three: entrenched conflicting narratives, the idealization of victimhood, and theological inhibitors to reconciliation.

"The first step is to open ourselves to listening to the stories of others," said one of the participants, and Musalaha is indeed making slow but steady progress in helping the two sides open up to the narratives they have chosen to ignore thus far. In our societies, we tend to entrench ourselves in our stories, just like Europe's World War I trenches that marked the de facto borders of a hopeless war with many casualties and little progress. However, when we as participants are willing to listen to and engage the other's narrative, it allows our own identity to be challenged, deconstructed, and nourished, and the futility of our deep trenches becomes evident. Again and again, the female interviewees pointed to the impact of one particular conference where they met with a Holocaust survivor and a Nakba refugee, and were greatly moved and challenged by their testimonies. Yet there is a long road ahead of us—we are still regularly offended by each other's framing stories and often by each other's expectations. Several of the women interviewed (from both sides) were put off by what they perceived as the other's expectation for them to accept guilt on the part of their nation or ancestors. I cannot help but wonder if this in itself is a form of dehumanization. In my opinion this reflects an attitude in which we see those we encounter as nations or ethno-religious groups instead of "*as* people." Instead of guilt, conviction, and apologies let us expect empathy, compassion, and social-action.

This deep desire to be apologized to is directly connected to the second barrier separating us—the idealization and prizing of victimhood. Sometimes it is as if the two sides are locked in a competition to prove who is the greater victim. This may seem somewhat odd and almost fetish-like to a Western observer of the conflict, yet one very important fact to remember is that both in Hebrew and in Arabic the word for "victim" is the same word as "sacrifice." In Western cultures, victimhood and sacrifice have been clearly distinguished from each other, but from a Semitic cultural-linguistic point of view they are one and the same. This idealization of victimhood can be even more exasperated in Christian and Messianic circles due to the centrality of Christ as our sacrifice/victim. I don't believe the solution is to impose a Western cultural-linguistic grid on the problem. Instead we have to carefully learn together how to be sacrificial *in the right way.* This seems to me to be one of the least explored concepts in regards to faith-based reconciliation in Israel and Palestine, and we must urgently engage it.

The third, and by far the most pronounced separation barrier, is in my opinion theological. On the Israeli side, one of the main inhibitors to reconciliation is the concept of Israel's theological uniqueness. This barrier is composed of two layers: firstly, the modern State of Israel is endowed with too much theological significance and secondly, Israel is treated by a different theological standard than other nations.

The first layer often occurs because Israeli Messianic Jews fail to distinguish between the *People of Israel* (the Jewish Nation) and the *State of Israel.* Moreover, in Hebrew (and Arabic) there is no artificial distinction between "Israelis" and "Israelites." Therefore, Messianic Jews commonly appropriate ancient prophecies of Israel's restoration to the modern State of Israel. It is important for me to stress that this is a legitimate, appropriate, and necessary exegesis, but it is equally important for me to stress that it is not the only exegesis which is appropriate and necessary. Almost all those prophecies originally refer to the restoration of Israel in the 6th and 5th centuries BC. Therefore, every application of those prophecies to current situations (and such applications are essential for the text to have any meaning for us today) are inevitably *midrashic.*

Midrash is a Jewish method of interpreting the Holy Scriptures which deliberately penetrates beyond the *p'shat* (the literal meaning of the text) and instead reads the text imaginatively by using word-play, allegory, and general inventiveness; this allows the text to speak into new situations and address new needs. If we Israeli Messianic Jews more consciously used this *midrashic* hermeneutic we would be less tempted to shoot down other applications of the prophetic texts which can speak hope to the Palestinian Nation; and if we remembered to distinguish between the Jewish *Nation* and Jewish *State*, we would be able to avoid erroneously confounding *liberty* with *sovereignty*, which unfortunately may actually get in the way of true liberty (e.g., the freedom from being oppressors).

The second layer of the theological barrier is to conclude that since Israel is theologically unique among the states of the world due to its divine origin and destiny, different rules apply to it. International law and standards of justice are pictured as man-made "humanist" concepts that contradict "God's justice," which is essentially equated with Israel doing whatever it needs to do to enhance its sovereignty over the land. Not all Messianics think this way, but if one is convinced of Israel's theological uniqueness, it is easy to come to these conclusions. However, this way of thinking flatly contradicts the vision of the Torah and Hebrew prophets (which ostensibly are the texts that justify this theology). In the Hebrew Scriptures, the Lord asserts that his concern for nations and lands extends beyond Israel, as he is the God that brought "Israel up from the land of Egypt, and the Philistines from Caphtor, and the Arameans from Kir" (Amos 9:7) and gave lands as an inheritance to the nations (Deut 2:9; 19; 22–23).

There are serious theological inhibitors on the Palestinian side as well. It seems to me that there are two basic theological tendencies among Palestinian Christians. The first tendency is to create a virtual dichotomy between issues of land and politics on the one side and spirituality and the Bible on the other side. This type of approach is detrimental not only to understanding the Messianic

Jewish perspective, and therefore to reconciliation, but also to the Palestinians themselves. If Palestinian Christians wish to effectively work towards holiness, justice, and peace in this land they must see *land* as something that has everything to do with spirituality and the Bible. I find hope in the fact that one Palestinian participant commented that "one of the most beautiful experiences was when we all shared communion together . . . You feel in that moment that you are one." When we, Jewish and Palestinian followers of the Messiah, share together in the Eucharist, the fruit of this land, we encounter together the crucified and risen Lord who is truly present in, through, and as the Eucharist, and are reconciled as one. Moreover, by sharing together bread and wine, we also share the *land* which we both love.

The second Palestinian tendency is to construct a theology which is all together reactionary and apologetic vis-à-vis the more dominant Messianic theologies of the land. Often these reactionary theologies do not generously deal with the needs and desires of the Jewish people. Some might even fall back into old Christian triumphalism that declares the Church to be *Verus Israel*, thus claiming all divine "chosenness" and viewing the non-Messianic Jews as divinely rejected. However, for any theology of reconciliation to be effective it must create spaces for Jews and Muslims, and affirm the ways in which they are chosen and their deep connections to this land.

Conflicting narratives, idealization of victimhood, and theologically driven inhibitions to reconciliation form a triple tiered Wall of Separation which seems to leave no room for peace. However, the last story in this book left me with hope as Yousef Khalil mischievously suggested: "You know Jericho? Maybe we can walk around this Wall seven times..." Maybe we can walk around this Wall of Separation *together*, not ignoring the issues, but rather tearing the Wall down simply by our togetherness and oneness as we walk. And if the Wall does not come tumbling down immediately, then at least we might be able to crack some window in it, and like Yousef, stand there, together, and shout: "Welcome!" We may all have slightly different understandings of justice, but we can all agree on the identity of the King "who is exalted in justice" (Isa 5:16), and together welcome Him as He returns to Zion.

SHIREEN HILAL

These stories in *Reflections* are simply that—reflections. But, they are not only reflections of the work Musalaha is doing, but also of the individual journeys each of the participants are encountering in their lives. It becomes clear to me as the stories are fleshed out that there is a difference, a huge difference between the Palestinian stories and the Israeli stories. This, I believe, is because we live in different societies, with distinct cultures and incomparable ways of life.

Musalaha over the years has struggled to gain acceptance from both the Israeli and Palestinian believing communities. Musalaha have been accused of being both pro-Palestinian and pro-Zionist, but we have a seen a change of heart over time. It was interesting how the statement, "we are one with Christ and that there is no conflict," was referenced and a theme throughout many of the stories. We are one in Christ, but there are issues we need to address. I do believe that Palestinian and Israeli believers try to hold to this motto, even if it is difficult to accept, to show that we are one in Christ, which brings people back. The fact that participants from both sides continue to come back is only evidence of the work and progress of Musalaha's Stages of Reconciliation.

The Stages of Reconciliation are the framework for which Musalaha takes its approach in addressing issues in this conflict. Stage one, is about building relationships. As women, this is where participants will retreat to when the stages become difficult; in stage two, they open up and share grievances and build further trust; but, it is in the third stage of the reconciliation process, the withdrawal stage, where people are challenged with reconciliation.

People start their reconciliation journey with excitement, enthusiasm, caution, hesitation, and curiosity. But, then each individual is met with grievances that they are unable to cope with and their relationships fade. But, it is not the end. Eventually participants return to the process because they know it is important and they move into the next stage of reclaiming their identity. They are committed and return even if it means taking risks. And eventually they take action together, confess, forgive, and attempt to bring about change.

I believe that the stories illustrate the process of reconciliation, though they do not explicitly state it. They prove that though they withdraw from the process, they are unwilling to reject it altogether. It is through these stages that Musalaha becomes more active. When grievance meets grievance, it is there we are reminded that we are one in Christ and it is critical that we move forward. We know that we are not alone in this process and we have brothers and sisters who are willing to help us along.

What is important and relayed through both the Israeli and Palestinian stories, is that we are not equal. The fact that we as Palestinians are separated by a Wall and our families are physically divided, shows that there is inequality. It was interesting that for Palestinians, the Wall is huge barrier that divides us physically, and we despise it. It was rarely mentioned and not emphasized enough as to how great an obstacle it has become in the daily lives of Palestinians. To look at this barrier every day of my life, it is an evident reminder of the things that physically divide us. As Palestinians, we are living under military occupation and it has caused many hurts and grievances.

This brings me to another point. Settlements. One Israeli mentions how a Palestinian woman came to visit her at her home in a so-called settlement. It is important that I emphasize, for Palestinians, even Palestinian Christians, the issue of settlements is non-negotiable. We do not accept the fact they live in settlements. For us it is not okay. As Palestinians, visiting our brothers and sisters in settlements is not because we accept the place where they are living, but because of our love for them as our brothers and sisters.

This then leads to the point, as shown throughout these stories, that there are two different issues for the two sides meeting. Palestinians are coming into the process because they want justice. They want people to apologize for the injustices incurred. However, upon entering into the reconciliation process they realize that the Israelis have difficulty understanding where they are coming from because they are approaching reconciliation from a theological standpoint. For Palestinians, our perception of Israel, before Musalaha, involved soldiers and checkpoints. And it has been distinctly negative. We have suffered frustration and humiliation.

Yet, through Musalaha as reflected in these stories we see that for many of our Israeli brothers and sisters, military service was not embraced as it is a required duty of the state. And, it is important to us that they did not embrace any of the cruel and humiliation actions, we as Palestinians have experienced as a result of this occupation.

While Palestinians demand justice, Israelis are coming into the reconciliation process from a theological perspective. "But I do believe Israel is God-ordained and we should be here. This is what God wants." I feel statements such as these justify the immoral actions of the state. This is a theology, most Palestinian Christians disagree with.

This, however, shows me that both sides are misled, whether it is a result of the media, their communities, or congregations. This is why the work of Musalaha is so important, even though it is not easy. Because Musalaha encounters many of the hindrances to reconciliation they are working hard to address the issues that separate the two communities. Some of the hindrances that Musalaha addresses includes un-forgiveness, bitterness, blame, denial, envy, hopelessness, control, hatred, injustice, and jealousy, "us" vs. "them" mentality, prejudice, resentment, and victimization. Seminars and training on these topics are always taught with the reminder of Jesus' teaching of reconciliation of love, peace, and tolerance.

In closing, I would like to reiterate what Pierre Tannous said in his story,

> Musalaha is not doing a work of just bringing people together and being happy. Musalaha doesn't take a position of judging which side is more right. It is just trying to get both sides to be open to the other side. When a person says they were treated inhumanely at the checkpoint, you can't say, "no you weren't." And when you say you are terrified from a suicide bombing attack you can't say "no you weren't." Israel is here and it's a historical fact. There were and are injustices, people losing water, and land, and we should speak about these things. But I don't want to connect this Israel to the Bible. It's here to stay, not because of the Bible. We need to let people from outside share in these experiences and let them decide where there is right and wrong.

We need to seek and reach out, even when it hurts the most in order to see the end of the road, but because it is a journey, we are moving at different paces and many times that requires patience and understanding.

Afterword

REFLECTING ON the stories in this volume, I am struck first of all by the courage of the individuals in the stories. To make a stand for reconciliation is to go against the grain, to fly in the face of inner-group pressure, and to encounter a known enemy. None of these are easily done, and all require a great deal of courage. Whatever impressions I have from reading these stories, or comments I have on their content should be understood in the context of the great respect I have for people in them. They all come from different backgrounds and different perspectives, and are all influenced by the conflict in a different way.

We should not underestimate the influence of a protracted, violent, and intractable conflict on individuals. Israelis and Palestinians are separated from each other, physically, emotionally, and spiritually, and while there are enormous social and political pressures pulling them away from each other, there is barely any incentive at all to reconcile. In the last twenty years, since Musalaha was founded, we have seen two *Intifadas*, numerous wars, and more political changes than I can count. All of these have made the task of reconciliation more difficult, but we have seen progress. It is clear from these stories that real friendships have developed between Israelis and Palestinians through Musalaha, and people on both sides have committed to walking the difficult road of reconciliation. Through these relationships, they have learned about each other, and are now able to contest prejudice in their own societies, to meet ignorance with knowledge. Attitudes have been changed, and consequently, behaviors have started to change as well.

This is all very positive, and these stories provide personal, human examples of Israelis and Palestinians crossing the cultural, linguistic, and national divide which can serve as a model to others who have not yet taken this step. However, from these stories it is evident that in one area we have encountered a problem: what do we do next? Over and over again, in these stories, and in the Musalaha events I have been able to attend, the same questions keep appearing, from both the Israelis and the Palestinians. They have established friendships with each other, and now they ask, "Where do we go from here?" This is an important question, but unfortunately there are no easy answers.

On the political front, there are many issues to take into consideration, settlements, and refugees, the borders, and Jerusalem just to name a few. But, since there is no consensus on how to deal with these complex issues, oftentimes they are avoided. Friendship is important, and vital if reconciliation is to occur. But for some of our participants, the friendships they have established through Musalaha actually prevent discussion of controversial issues. They do not want to discuss something when they know they will disagree, and possibly fight. They fear that this may hurt their friendship.

While we should have respect for each other, and should avoid deliberate antagonism, we cannot allow our friendship to stand in the way of an open, honest, and painful (if need be) discussion of the conflict and the issues that come with it. In fact, we should discuss these issues *because* of our friendship. In the context of friendship a meaningful discussion is possible, whereas if the foundation of friendship does not exist, people will rarely even listen to each other. If we truly are brothers and sisters, one body of the Messiah and one family, then we should not be afraid of confrontation. Families always fight, but they remain family no matter what. A unifying love holds them together.

Another thing that struck me while reading these stories was how different the challenges were for the Israelis and Palestinians. For example, the Palestinians interviewed seemed to focus on the political situation, specifically on the occupation. Their stories speak about the daily struggles they face, the checkpoints, the settlements, and their contact with the army. They appreciate the friendships they have made with Israelis, but for them the fellowship is not enough, they want to see a change. Their situation is bad and they want to see it improved. There is an urgency to this feeling, especially for the Christians, since their situation is arguably worse than the situation faced by the Muslim Palestinians. They are a double minority, living between two majorities, the Jewish, and the Muslim. The gravity of their situation is seen in the waves of Palestinian Christian emigration leaving the country.

For the Messianic Jewish Israelis, the affect of these meetings is no less impactful, but markedly different. For most of them, the emphasis seems to be on theology, specifically the disparity between their theological beliefs concerning the land of Israel and its promises, and the things that they see and hear from the Palestinian brothers and sisters. This problem arises because of their sincere desire to have friendship and fellowship with their new Palestinian friends, and the sincerity of their beliefs and convictions. But what is to be done if they do not correlate? Especially since many of them have invested an enormous amount of time and energy, a lifetime commitment, into the concept of supporting Israel as the home of the Jewish people. For some of them, this theological conviction motivated their immigration to Israel in the first place. Therefore, to have it challenged can be very threatening, and understandably traumatic. But they are increasingly becoming aware of the fact that they need to take into account the Palestinian people, and must have room in their theology for the Palestinian Christians.

Obviously, there is a great deal of pain and hurt on both sides, and both of them desire an end to the conflict. However, one does get the sense from reading these stories that for the Palestinians it is a more pressing issue. This would explain why the Palestinians do seem to press harder for discussion of the difficult and divisive issues. They often come to the meetings with a list of grievances, and attempt to correct the imbalance of power that leans in favor of the Israelis in the political and economic sphere. This also explains why many of the Israelis come out of these meetings feeling guilty, and as though they have been accused of some great crime. They feel that they are being personally blamed for all the suffering that the Palestinians endure, and this is not easy for them at all. Some of them withdraw from the process at this point, because they do not see why they should keep meeting with Palestinians and keep being made to feel this guilt. The difficulties do not end there, for even if the Israelis do chose to stay involved beyond this point, and want to address the imbalance of power, they encounter opposition from the Palestinians who are not interested in charity or a hand-out. They want to see change on the political front.

The issue of justice has come up repeatedly, especially among the Palestinian participants. We have always considered this an important aspect of reconciliation, but recently we have tried to address it in a more direct way. Musalaha is currently creating a curriculum for reconciliation, which deals extensively with justice, and is attempting to develop a theology of reconciliation, which will incorporate justice, as well as mercy, peace, and love, and see the cry for justice in the context of the cross. These stories serve as good motivation, and they point to the problematic issues from both sides.

Another challenge that has become more significant in recent years is the rise of radicalism among the different religious groups involved in the conflict. In both camps, religion has replaced nationalism, to a certain extent, and the tendency among those who adhere to religious radicalism is to speak in the uncompromising language of absolutes. This radicalism on both sides has also become a significant block to reconciliation on a broader scale. For example, a Palestinian might say "I have no problem with my

Israeli brother, and we have fellowship through Musalaha encounters, but how can there ever be peace when the settlers continue to steal our land?" Similarly, Israelis could say "I am thankful for my friendship with our Palestinian Christian brothers and sisters, but the conflict will never end unless their leaders reject radical Islam and terrorist tactics."

On an emotional level, we see that the Israelis tend to operate out of fear, and the Palestinians out of anger. For the Israelis, it is a fear, on the one hand, of terror attacks and acts of violence that have plagued Israeli society from the time it was established until today. On the other hand, it is a fear of reliving the expulsions, pogroms, and genocide that the Jewish people have faced throughout their long history. The Palestinian's anger also has two parts: first, it is the anger that is the natural result of having experienced a traumatic and destructive blow, of seeing a whole society and way of life uprooted and destroyed. It is the anger of the long history of abuses and injustice suffered, and of muffled anger left with no avenue of expression. Second, it is the anger which results from seeing the current situation, and feeling as though nothing has changed.

These two emotions are always so clearly observed when one encounters a group of foreign pilgrims from the United States or Europe. Their behavior and attitude will inform you right away of who they spent their time with. If they are obsessed with security, and paranoid about radical Islam, they probably spent their time with Israelis. If they seem filled with righteous indignation, full of condemnation for the support their own country provides Israel, and mention "The Wall," they have most likely visited with Palestinians. Fear and anger, two emotions that are perfectly natural, but can be destructive when taken to the extreme.

Reading over these stories has been a sobering experience for me, especially as Director of Musalaha. I feel challenged by the words of some of the participants, as well as those who offered their reflections. It is clear that we still have much ground to cover;

our journey is far from over. There is, however, a very vivid, discernable element of hope in these stories, which has encouraged me a great deal. Recently, we hosted a woman's conference on the topic of The Nakba and the Shoah (Holocaust). It was a very intense conference, which challenged many of the women, and upset more than a few of them. We received a lot of criticism for even approaching this topic, and had to seriously reevaluate our strategy. But then, as I read these stories, so many of the women commented on how important that conference was. It seems as though it did upset them, but with time they came to realize that it was an important topic to discuss. It stayed with them. Even though it was intense, and tested the strength of the women's friendships, they survived it, and their friendship's survived as well.

This is not to say that the women agreed on everything, but they were able to discuss it openly. This is the essence of reconciliation, to embrace the other, the enemy, in love, for "Whoever does not love does not know God, because God is love." Furthermore, "If anyone says 'I love God,' yet hates his brother, he is a liar. For anyone who does not love his brother, whom he has seen, cannot love God, whom he has not seen. And he has given this command: Whoever loves God must also love his brother." (1 John 4:8, 20–21) It has been inspirational to read these stories, and join the participants as they walk down the path of reconciliation. It is a narrow path, and hard to follow, but in the end it leads to healing. All other paths lead to destruction. We invite others to join us on this path toward reconciliation.

SALIM J. MUNAYER
Musalaha Director